POWER WRITING

Writing Effective Sentences

CAMBRIDGE ADULT EDUCATION

A Division of Simon & Schuster

Upper Saddle River, New Jersey

Executive Editor: Mark Moscowitz

Project Editors: Karen Bernhaut, Douglas Falk, Amy Jolin, Kristen Shepos-Salvatore

Series Editor: Michael Buchman

Development Editor: Mary McGarry

Writer: Michael Buchman

Production Editor: Alan Dalgleish

Art Director: Pat Smythe

Interior Design and Electronic Page Production: Margarita Giammanco

Marketing Manager: Will Jarred

Cover Design: Sheree Goodman Designs

Printed in the United States of America

1 2 3 4 5 6 7 8 9 10   99 98 97 96 95

ISBN 0-8359-4662-2

CAMBRIDGE ADULT EDUCATION
A Division of Simon & Schuster
Upper Saddle River, New Jersey

Contents

To the Student

What is Power Writing?

Power Writing is a series of four books that help you build your writing skills. Every chapter begins with a real-life situation involving people you might find in your neighborhood. The skills you learn in the lessons and exercises will begin your preparation for the Graduate Equivalency Degree (GED) Writing Test. Each chapter ends with writing assignments that apply the skills from the lessons and relate to the life skills introduced at the beginning of the chapter.

The first two books help strengthen your grammatical knowledge and sentence-writing skills. You will develop an editing checklist, and you will begin using the techniques of the writing process to build a portfolio.

The last two books focus on the writing process and help you write more effective paragraphs and essays. You will also review grammatical skills as you revise and edit the work in your growing portfolio.

The contents of each book shows the skills presented. These skills were carefully selected and coordinated with the Test of Adult Basic Education (TABE). The Life Skill themes are based on the Comprehensive Adult Student Assessment System (CASAS).

How do you get started? Identify the appropriate book for your skill level by taking the Locator Test found in the Instructor's Guide. You may choose to review material that you already know. In each chapter you will:

- Read the opening story and study the Key Terms and Life Skill Words.
- Complete short lessons and exercises.
- Work on writing assignments designed to:
  - Build your vocabulary and use the glossary.
  - Read and write about related ideas.
  - Establish a writing portfolio.

Use the Answer Key at the back of each book to check your work after you have completed all the questions in an exercise. Ask your instructor to explain any answer you don't understand.

The Writing Process

Good writers take risks. Good writers are rewriters. Good writers become good editors. Through the activities in these books you will progress through clear stages: prewriting and idea generation, drafting, revising, editing, and publishing.

Good writers also know that writing is thinking. As you develop your ideas you will move back and forward through the writing process until your thoughts are clearly communicated.

As you work through each book in this series you will see your power to communicate grow. This power will help you in your daily life and in your continuing education.

Chapter 1

Simple Sentences

Anna loved her new apartment. The neighborhood was safer, too. The only problem was that she did not feel as if she belonged yet. "I'll just have to start exploring!" she thought.

Here was Anna's **plan**: First, she **analyzed**, or thought about, her situation. What did she enjoy in her old community that she might also enjoy here? Reading with her four-year-old, Martin, was very important to her. She also liked listening to music and being with people.

Then, she needed **information**. How, when, and where could she enjoy all these things and not spend a lot of money? Like most, her family was on a budget.

The solution to Anna's problem was just a telephone call away. She used the **telephone book** to find the number of her local **government**. A **government guide** was listed in the **blue pages** at the back of the book. Anna was amazed at how many **departments** were listed, all in **alphabetical order**. She was not sure which one to call so she dialed the general information number.

Anna learned that the **library** was a short walk away. It had a story hour for young children where she would meet other parents, too. Free puppet shows for kids were planned for the summer. Anna would have no trouble fitting in.

Key Terms

- capitalize
- declarative sentence
- exclamatory sentence
- fragment
- imperative sentence
- interrogative sentence
- punctuation mark
- sentence
- subject
- thought completer
- verb

Life Skill Words

- alphabetical order
- analyzed
- blue pages
- departments
- government
- government guide
- information
- library
- plan
- telephone book

What Is a Sentence

Whether you are speaking or writing, the most important thing is for you to be understood. The truth is, though, that you have a much better chance of being understood when you speak. Why? You can use your eyes, your facial expressions, your voice, and your gestures—your body language—to make your message clear and complete.

When you write, however, you have to be more exact. No one is looking at you. They see only the words that you write. To make sure that your readers understand your message, you will have to write groups of words that are clear and complete.

Look at the following two groups of words. Which one tells you more about the message?

"Need the telephone book for Benjamin."

"I need to use the telephone book to call Benjamin."

The second group of words not only gives you more information than the first group of words, the *meaning* of the second group of words also is clearer. The second group of words is a sentence.

A **sentence** is a group of words that express a complete thought. If a group of words does not express a complete thought, it is called a **fragment**. Here are more examples of sentences:

Does the new employee need help?
NOT: Need help?

The plan went into effect yesterday.
NOT: Yesterday.

We had better obey the law!
NOT: Better obey!

If only you knew about the traffic, you would have left earlier.
NOT: If you knew about the traffic.

Write *S* in the blank lines if the following groups of words are sentences. Write *F* in the blank lines if the groups of words are fragments. An example is done for you.

Example: __F__ Whenever I like.

____ 1. Coming over?

____ 2. Matthew will go to the outdoor concert.

____ 3. Ms. Ortiz visited the library.

____ 4. Since your supervisor wants the information in alphabetical order.

____ 5. Didn't know that.

____ 6. Your idea is so creative!

____ 7. Is the newspaper delivered daily?

____ 8. Need the report by Monday.

____ 9. Now the banks are open on Saturdays.

____ 10. Of course.

Check your answers on page 95.

Subjects and Verbs

To be complete, a sentence must have two parts: (1) a subject and (2) a verb.

SUBJECTS

A **subject** names someone or something. The subject of a sentence names (1) a person, (2) a place, (3) a thing, (4) an idea, or (5) a feeling.

To find the subject, read the sentence and then ask yourself these questions: *Who or what is doing the action? Who or what is the action done to?* Keep these questions in mind as you identify the SUBJECTS, which are in capital letters, in the following sentences:

That CUSTOMER likes the mall.

Who likes the mall? A person *(customer)* likes the mall.

The MEETING lasted all morning.

What lasted all morning? A thing *(meeting)* lasted all morning.

The OFFICE is downtown.

What is downtown? A place *(office)* is downtown.

COURTESY becomes important on the job.

What is important? An idea *(courtesy)* is important.

FEAR overcame the guests.

What overcame the guests? A feeling *(fear)* overcame the guests.

Here is another clue you can use to identify the parts of a sentence: The subject is often—*but not always*—the first word in the sentence.

Exercise 1.2a

Write the subjects of the following sentences in the space provided. An example is done for you.

Example: __Anna__ Anna likes her music loud.

_____	1. Safety comes first when driving a car.
_____	2. The chart shows all the baseball scores.
_____	3. Alaska has cold weather.
_____	4. The lifeguards practiced their strokes.
_____	5. Happiness filled our hearts.
_____	6. This information caused an uproar.
_____	7. The painters worked on the building today.
_____	8. City Hall was busy during tax season.
_____	9. The kindness of Karen touched everyone.
_____	10. Monday night's concert attracted hundreds of people.

Check your answers on page 95.

VERBS

The subject, as you know, tells *who* or *what* the sentence is about. The **verb** tells you something about the subject. A verb is usually—*but not always*—close to the subject of a sentence. It expresses (1) a physical action, (2) a mental action, or (3) a feeling. A verb also can make a statement about a subject.

To find the verb, read a sentence and ask yourself these questions: *What is the subject physically doing, mentally doing, or feeling? What statement is being made about the subject?* Keep these questions in mind as you identify the verbs, which are underlined, in the same sentences we already wrote:

The MEETING <u>lasted</u> all morning.

What is the subject *physically doing?* The meeting *lasted.*

FEAR <u>overcame</u> the guests.

What is the subject *mentally doing?* Fear *overcame* the guests.

That CUSTOMER <u>likes</u> the mall.

What is the subject *feeling?* The customer *likes* the mall.

The OFFICE <u>is</u> downtown.

What statement is being made about the subject? The office *is* downtown.

COURTESY <u>becomes</u> important on the job.

What statement is being made about the subject? Courtesy *becomes* important.

Exercise 1.2b

Underline the verbs in the following sentences. An example is done for you.

Example: Anna <u>finds</u> services in the telephone book.

1. The library installed new shelves.
2. Tony registered to vote today.
3. Boston is a famous American city.
4. Her thoughtfulness made that manager popular.
5. Cindy checked the phone book first.
6. The employees agreed to leave on time.
7. Our neighbors traveled 800 miles by bus.
8. The newcomers hated the cold weather.
9. Savona applied for a job.
10. Impatience when standing in a long line is understandable.

Check your answers on page 95.

Thought Completers

If you reread the sentences we used in Lessons 2 and 3, you will see that they include more than just subjects and verbs. These extra words make the sentence's message complete. A word or group of words that completes the meaning of a sentence is called a **thought completer**.

Ask yourself the following question: *Is the sentence clear and complete with just a subject and verb?* If it isn't, look for the sentence's thought completer. A thought completer usually—*but not always*—is at the end of the sentence.

As you can see, we would not be able to understand most of our sentences without their *thought completers,* which are italicized:

Incomplete: That CUSTOMER <u>likes</u>.

Complete: That CUSTOMER <u>likes</u> *the mall.*

| Incomplete: | The OFFICE <u>is</u>. |
| Complete: | The OFFICE <u>is</u> *downtown*. |

| Incomplete: | COURTESY <u>becomes</u>. |
| Complete: | COURTESY <u>becomes</u> *important on the job*. |

| Incomplete: | FEAR <u>overcame</u>. |
| Complete: | FEAR <u>overcame</u> *the guests*. |

The only sentence in our examples that didn't need a thought completer was this one:

| Complete: | The MEETING <u>lasted</u>. |
| Complete: | The MEETING <u>lasted</u> all morning |

Even though "all morning" is part of this sentence, this group of words is not necessary to make the sentence complete. These words do add important detail, though.

Exercise 1.3

If the following items are sentences, write *OK* in the space provided. If they need thought completers to become sentences, write *TC* in the space provided. An example is done for you.

Example: __TC__ The book contained.

_____ 1. The catalog listed.
_____ 2. Jessica's trip was great.
_____ 3. Mr. Anderson's nervousness made the audience jumpy.
_____ 4. His health actually improved.
_____ 5. The police officer filed.
_____ 6. The minister seemed.
_____ 7. The plan is considered.
_____ 8. Ohio's senators both voted against the plan.
_____ 9. The television on the cart cost.
_____ 10. She dialed a wrong number.

Check your answers on page 95.

Capitalizing and Punctuating Types of Sentences

The first word in a sentence is **capitalized** (KAP-eh-tuhl-eyezd). Since an uppercase (or capital) letter is written larger than a lowercase letter, it marks the beginning of the complete thought. A **punctuation mark** (puhnk-chuh-WAY-shuhn mahrk) like a period (.), question mark (?), or exclamation point (!) indicates the end of the thought and the sentence.

Exercise 1.4a

Read the following paragraph. If a sentence is correct, write *OK* in the numbered space below. If a sentence is not correct, make it correct by capitalizing the first word in the sentence in the numbered space. The first one is done for you.

(1) applying for a library card was easy! (2) Anna and Martin walked to the local branch on Saturday. (3) "How do we get library cards?" (4) Mrs. Pinto, the librarian, smiled and asked for identification. (5) "all I need is proof that you live here," she explained. (6) "but we just moved here!" (7) "do you have a driver's license or some mail with your address on it?" (8) "show Mrs. Pinto our gas bill," Anna said to Martin. (9) anna was congratulating herself for making that telephone call before coming, when Mrs. Pinto spoke again. (10) "Welcome to our library family!"

1. <u> Applying </u>
2. _____
3. _____
4. _____
5. _____
6. _____
7. _____
8. _____
9. _____
10. _____

Check your answers on page 95.

Sentences can do several things. A **declarative** (duh-KLAIR-uh-tihv) **sentence** states a fact or an opinion or describes something. A declarative sentence ends with a period (.).

Declarative Sentences

Fact:	Her telephone number was listed incorrectly.
Opinion:	She tries to be a good mother.
Description:	She looked worried.

An **imperative** (ihm-PEHR-uh-tihv) **sentence** states an order, command, or request. It can end in a period or exclamation mark (!) depending on the tone of the speaker. An imperative sentence does not name the subject. Instead, it implies the subject is you.

Imperative Sentences

Normal Tone:	Let me have the egg salad special.
	Please go home.
Strong Tone:	Go home now!

An **interrogative** (ihn-ter-RAHG-uh-tihv) **sentence** asks a question and ends in a question mark (?). Questions often begin with the words *Who, What, Where, When, Why,* and *How.*

Sometimes questions are formed by reversing the order of the subject and a helping verb like *will, can, do, may, would, could, did,* or *might.*

You can also form a question by simply adding a question mark to a declarative sentence. This form can add a little surprise or uncertainty to the tone of the question, depending on how it is said.

Interrogative Sentences

Question words:	What time does the library open?
	When does it close?
	How many books can I take out?
Reversed subject-verb order:	Did you find the library?
	Will I like it?
	Could we go there together?
Question mark alone:	You found the library?
	I'll like it?
	We could go there together?

An **exclamatory** (ehks-KLAM-uh-taw-ree) **sentence** expresses great surprise or emotion. These sentences end in exclamation marks (!). If you use a period instead of an exclamation mark, the sentence becomes declarative.

Exclamatory Sentences

Emotion:	Martin loved the story hour!
Surprise:	They had many children's books!

Exercise 1.4b

Reread the paragraph in Exercise 1.4a. This time, use the space provided to identify the types of sentences. Write *DEC* for declarative, *INT* for interrogative, *IMP* for imperative, and *EXC* for exclamatory. The first one is done for you.

1. _____EXC_____
2. _____
3. _____
4. _____
5. _____
6. _____
7. _____
8. _____
9. _____
10. _____

Check your answers on page 95.

Exercise 1.4c

Add the missing punctuation marks to the end of the following sentences. If the first word of a sentence is not capitalized, rewrite it correctly in the space provided. An example is done for you.

Example: you can't be serious _!_ _____You_____

1. I like reading magazines__ _____
2. give Janet the keys to the house__ _____
3. Where is Rico's baseball glove__ _____
4. The cashier packed the old man's groceries__ _____
5. I can't believe it__ _____
6. how much more money do we need to save__ _____
7. Walk down this street for two blocks and turn left onto Dunlap Road__ _____
8. most people in the library enjoyed the air conditioning__ _____
9. You absolutely must stop bothering your brother right now__ _____
10. Do the blue pages list government agencies__ _____

Check your answers on page 95.

Simple Sentences

Building Your Word Power

Words stand for ideas. The more words you know and use, the better you can express yourself. You will think more clearly, and people will understand you better. You learn to use words correctly by reading and writing regularly. With practice your writing power will grow.

To start a Word Notebook of vocabulary and spelling words:

- When you read, use a dictionary to look up hard words. Add these words to your notebook.

- Be sure to spell new words correctly in your notebook. Check that every letter is present and in the right order. Double-check. You don't want to study the *wrong* spelling.

- If a word's meaning is new to you, include a definition and an example in your notebook.

Assignment: Start a Word Notebook today.

- Include the Key Terms and Life Skill Words from this chapter.
- Break each word into syllables.
- Write an original sentence for at least five of the words.

Example:

information   in-for-ma-tion

The telephone book has lots of useful information.

Reading to Write

Clip or photocopy an announcement of a community event from your local newspaper. Paste it in your word notebook. Add at least two words to your word notebook from the announcement.

Building Your Writing Power

"Freewriting" is a way to get your writing creativity flowing. Forget about spelling and grammar for now. Just have fun! Trust your feelings and your ideas. Pick one of these topics and spend at least five minutes writing sentences about it:

- Using the telephone book to get information
- Making a request over the telephone
- How you feel about your library

Chapter 2

Repairing Fragments

When his church decided to throw a carnival to raise money, Jaime Bolivar said he'd help with **publicity**. Jaime knew the public library had a **community bulletin board**, so he called in the middle of the day.

He was surprised when he got a recording. "Welcome to your public library. This is the **voice mail** system. If you know the number of the **extension** you need, enter it followed by the **pound key** at any time during this message. Our regular operating hours are: Monday to Friday, 10 A.M. . . . ," the pleasant voice went on and on.

"I wonder how you get to talk to a person," Jaime thought. "And what the heck is a 'pound key'?"

"For a listing of **options**, please press '3' and the **star key** . . ." the voice continued.

"What have I got to lose?" Jaime mumbled as he pressed the number. "I'm bound to find somebody alive down there soon."

Key Terms

- complex sentence
- dependent clause
- direct object
- editing
- fragment
- helping verb
- independent clause
- portfolio
- predicate
- predicate adjective
- predicate nominative

Life Skill Words

- community bulletin board
- extension
- options
- pound key
- publicity
- star key
- voice mail

Recognizing Fragments

As you learned in Chapter 1, a **fragment** is a group of words that does not express a complete thought. A fragment may begin with a capitalized word and end with a period, but it is not a sentence.

People use fragments in everyday speech, but good writers are careful to use complete sentences. That way readers can understand their meaning more fully. Fragments often leave you asking questions.

When a fragment is missing a *subject,* you probably wonder *who* or *what* the writer is talking about.

> FRAGMENT: Heard this message before.
>
> (*Who* heard the message?)

> FRAGMENT: Was becoming urgent.
>
> (*What* was becoming urgent?)

When a fragment is missing a *verb,* you are left asking, *What action* did the subject take? or *What about* the subject?

> FRAGMENT: The message about the libarary hours.
>
> (*What about* the message?)

> FRAGMENT: Jaime's publicity committee.
>
> (*What action* did the committee take?)

Some verbs need a *thought completer* to describe or rename the subject, or to tell what was acted upon.

> FRAGMENT: The recording seemed.
>
> (*How* did the recording seem?)

> FRAGMENT: The regular hours were.
>
> (*What* were the hours?)

> FRAGMENT: Yesterday Jaime needed.
>
> (*What* did he need?)

Exercise 2.1

Read each numbered item. If it is a sentence, write *sentence* in the space. If it is a fragment, write the word *fragment* and explain what is missing. Then write a question that the fragment fails to answer. An example is done for you.

Example: At the library's reference desk. __fragment—Both subject__
__and verb are missing. Who or what did what at the desk?__

1. Today Jaime and the librarian. _____

_____

2. Spoke about the carnival. _____

_____

3. They talked for some time. _____

_____

4. The glass-covered community bulletin board. _____

_____

5. Seemed half empty. _____

_____

6. The notice was short. _____

_____

7. From a distance, the notice looked. _____

_____

8. Discussed the phone system. _____

_____

9. The "pound key" is to the right of the "zero" key. _____

_____

10. The "star key" is. _____

_____

Check your answers on page 96.

Adding Thought Completers

A fragment may have a subject and a verb, but still fail to complete a thought. The verb *to be (am, are, is, was, were)* usually needs a thought completer. So do other linking verbs like *seem, look, become,* and *feel.*

The verb and its thought completer is sometimes called the **predicate** (PREHD-ih-kuht) of a sentence. A noun or pronoun that names, identifies, or stands for the subject is called a **predicate nominative** (NAHM-nuht-ihv). An adjective in the predicate that describes the subject is called a **predicate adjective**.

Fragment	*Thought Completer*
Jaime is	a busy <u>man</u>. (predicate nominative) *who, what.*
Estelle was	<u>busy</u> too. (predicate adjective)
Jaime and Estelle became	close <u>friends</u>. (predicate nominative)
They look	<u>happy</u>. (predicate adjective)

Some verbs need a **direct object**, a noun or pronoun for the subject to act upon. Without this object the thought cannot be complete. Each of the underlined nouns is a direct object.

Fragment	*Thought Completer*
Jaime called	the <u>editor</u>.
She sent	a <u>reporter</u>.
The newspaper covered	the <u>carnival</u>. /ˈkɔːnəvl/ n. 嘉年华会 (四月斋前之狂宴纵乐)
The writer liked	the <u>music</u>.
The church needed	the <u>publicity</u>.
They raised	<u>$2300</u>.

Exercise 2.2a

Read each numbered item. If it is a sentence, write *Sentence* in the space. If it is a fragment, rewrite it and add a thought completer. An example is done for you.

Example: Voice mail seemed. _____Voice mail seemed complicated. a. 复杂的____

1. The instructions were. ____clearly____

n.教授.教导 例.指令

optimism n. 乐观. 乐观义
optimist n 乐观义者.
optimistic a.

2. Jaime felt. _____ well _____

_____

3. He replayed his message. _____ ✓ _____

_____

4. His voice sounded. _____ pleasure _____

_____

5. The library director saw. _____

_____

Check your answers on page 96.

Exercise 2.2b

The following items contain subjects. Make each subject into two different *complete* sentences: the first by adding a *verb only,* the second by adding *verb and a thought completer.* An example is done for you.

Example: The church's old answering machine

Add a verb: _____ The church's old answering macine broke. _____

Add a verb and a thought completer: _____ The church's old answering _____ machine picked up my call _____

1. The library's reference desk

Add a verb: _____ is helpful . _____

Add a verb and a thought completer: _____ helps people . _____

_____

2. The huge dictionary on the wooden stand

Add a verb: _____ fell _____

Add a verb and a thought completer: _____ is popular _____

_____

3. The newspaper reporter

Add a verb: _____

Add a verb and a thought completer: _____

4. The children playing basketball

   Add a verb: _____

   Add a verb and a thought completer: _____

   _____

5. Jaime's dog, Ralph

   Add a verb: _____

   Add a verb and a thought completer: _____

   _____

Check your answers on page 96.

Adding Subjects and Verbs

When a fragment begins with a verb, you need to add a subject. Sometimes you need to add a helping verb, as well. A **helping verb** completes a verb phrase helping to change the tense. Some helping verbs include will, forms of the verb to be (am, are, was, were), and forms of the verb to have (have, has, had).

Subjects and Helping Verbs	*Fragments*
We were	talking to store owners about the carnival.
Jaime has	been out delivering posters since noon.
Mr. Sanchez is	returning Jaime's call.
He will be	putting up the poster tomorrow.

Exercise 2.3

Write a sentence using each fragment below. Add a subject (or a subject and helping verb) to make your sentences complete. An example is done for you.

Example: Looking down the street. <u>She was looking down the street.</u>

1. heard the carnival parade around the corner. _____

   _____

2. carrying banners and flags. _____

   11. 旗帜，根据以大有题

3. set up the food booths. _____

_____

4. played music in the street until dark. _____

_____

5. eaten more than I should have. _____

_____

Check your answers on page 96.

Using Commas

An **independent clause** can stand alone. It can be a complete sentence. A **dependent clause** contains a subject and a verb, but it cannot stand alone as a sentence. It depends on an independent clause to make complete sense. Dependent clauses begin with words that link them to other ideas. When those ideas are missing, the clause remains as a fragment.

Because the church helped the people in his community.

If Jaime was convincing.

After Estelle saw his hard work.

When she finished her shift at the bakery.

One way to turn a dependent clause into a sentence is to simply remove the first word.

The church helped the people in his community.

Jaime was convincing.

Estelle saw his hard work.

She finished her shift at the bakery.

Most of the time, however, those words are important. You want to connect the dependent clause to another sentence. That will show the relationship between two sets of ideas. In the following examples the independent clause is underlined. Notice that this clause could stand as a sentence.

Jaime worked on the carnival because the church helped the people in his community.

If Jaime was convincing, the owner agreed to display a poster in the store window.

Estelle liked him even more after she saw his hard work.

When she finished her shift at the bakery, she helped at the game booths.

When a dependent clause comes first in a sentence, it is followed by a comma. No comma is used between clauses when the independent clause comes first.

A sentence that includes both an independent clause and a dependent clause is called a **complex sentence**. You will study complex sentences further in chapters 5 and 6.

Exercise 2.4

Rewrite each fragment as a sentence by adding an independent clause to the dependent clauses. If the dependent clause comes first, be sure to insert a comma before the independent clause. Add correct capitalization and punctuation. An example is done for you.

Example: when Jaime called the library When Jaime called the library, he reached the voice mail system.

1. because the voice mail system offered a long list of options _____

   _____

2. since Jaime got confused _____

   _____

3. although Jaime was patient _____

   _____

4. if Jaime called back _____

   _____

5. before he called back _____

   _____

6. since he pressed the "2" key _____

   _____

7. when Jaime finally spoke to a live person _____

8. after Jaime hung up _____

_____

9. if I had known all this would happen _____

_____

10. although when I wrote down the options _____

_____

Check your answers on page 96.

Writing Assignments

Building Your Writing Power: Start a Writing Portfolio

A **portfolio** is a collection of your writing, notes, and the information you gather. Use a folder or a notebook to store these materials. Store your "freewriting" assignment from Chapter 1 in your portfolio. You will add to your portfolio throughout this book.

Beginning an Editing Checklist

Editing means improving the way something is written. People usually reread what they have written. They often add, cut, or change words. They correct errors in spelling and in the way words are used. An editing checklist includes things to look for when you reread your writing.

Directions: Write "Editing Checklist" at the top of a blank page. Write the following items in a list down the left side of the page. You will keep this checklist in your portfolio and add to it in the following chapters.

- A sentence must express a complete thought.
- A sentence must include a subject, verb, and often a thought completer.
- A fragment is not a complete thought because it leaves the reader with important questions.
- A dependent clause contains a subject and verb, but begins with a word that could link it to another sentence.
- A dependent clause is a fragment. Either drop its first word, or connect it to another complete sentence.

Use your editing checklist to improve the sentences in your portfolio.

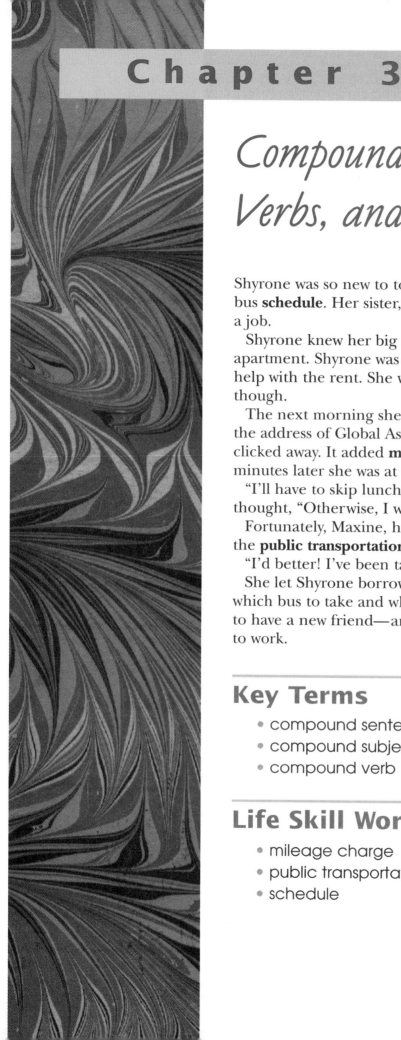

Chapter 3

Compound Subjects, Verbs, and Sentences

Shyrone was so new to town that she hadn't even picked up a bus **schedule**. Her sister, Vivian, however, already had found her a job.

Shyrone knew her big sister was glad to be sharing an apartment. Shyrone was grateful to have a job, too, so she could help with the rent. She wasn't sure how she would get to work, though.

The next morning she called a taxi cab and gave the driver the address of Global Assembly. The **taxi meter** turned on and clicked away. It added **mileage charges** as they went. Twenty minutes later she was at work and $10 poorer.

"I'll have to skip lunch *and* ask for bus directions," she thought, "Otherwise, I won't get home."

Fortunately, Maxine, her partner on the assembly line, knew the **public transportation** system well.

"I'd better! I've been taking it all my life."

She let Shyrone borrow her bus **timetable**. She explained which bus to take and where to **transfer**. Shyrone was relieved to have a new friend—and a reliable and affordable way to get to work.

Key Terms

- compound sentence
- compound subject
- compound verb
- conjunction
- conjunction pair
- run-on sentence

Life Skill Words

- mileage charge
- public transportation
- schedule
- taxi meter
- timetable
- transfer

Compound Subjects

Often, the subject of a sentence is the noun or pronoun performing an action. Two or more nouns can perform the same action, of course. They might also be identified or described together.

> Maxine _or_ Shyrone works overtime on Wednesday.
>
> Shyrone _and_ I are sisters.

In the examples above the underlined words are **compound subjects**, two or more nouns or pronouns acting as the subject of a sentence. Notice that _either_ Maxine _or_ Shyrone perform the same action: Either one _works overtime on Wednesday._ Likewise, _both_ Shyrone _and_ I are identified the same way: They _are sisters._

JOINING SUBJECTS WITH _AND_

When a subject is formed with _and,_ it is treated as a plural. A "joining" word like _and_ is called a **conjunction.** You can emphasize the joining of two nouns by using the **conjunction pair** _both . . . and._

> _Both_ Shyrone _and_ Vivian are hard workers.
>
> _Both_ the bus _and_ the train go uptown.

The first sentence emphasizes that both people in the compound subject are hard workers. Similarly, the second sentence emphasizes that both kinds of transportation go uptown. You could substitute a plural pronoun, _they,_ for these compound subjects:

> They both _are_ hard workers.
>
> They both _go_ uptown.

Notice that the verbs <u>underlined twice</u> in both these examples are plural.

JOINING SUBJECTS WITH _OR_

When a compound subject is formed with _or,_ it is treated as a singular. The conjunction _or_ means that _either_ subject element (but not both) performs the action or fits the description. You can emphasize this choice by using the conjunction pair _either . . . or ._

> The bus _or_ the train is cheaper than a taxi.
>
> _Either_ Maxine _or_ the supervisor helps new workers.

In both cases the verb agrees with the singular subject.

Either Mary or Jane is coming.

Either Tom or his friends are coming.

Either his friends or Tom is coming.

非正原则).
= neither...nor...

Read each pair of sentences. Then rewrite them as a single sentence, using the conjunction in parentheses to form a compound subject. Underline the compound subject once and the verb twice. An example is done for you.

Example: (and) Vivian shops for groceries. Shyrone shops for groceries.
<u>Vivian and Shyrone</u> <u>shop</u> for groceries.

1. (either . . . or) Vivian will carry the packages home. Shyrone will carry the packages home.

   Either Vivian or Shyrone will carry the packages home.

   _____

2. (and) Emery lives near the bus stop. Shyrone lives near the bus stop.

   Emery and Shyrone live near the bus stop.

   _____

3. (both . . . and) Emery likes listening to live music. Shyrone likes listening to live music.

   Both Emery and Shyrone like listening to live music.

   _____

4. (or) Emery was starting to speak. Shyrone was starting to speak.

   Emery or Shyrone was starting to speak.

   _____

5. (and) Emery was grinning. I was grinning.

   Emery and I were grinning.

   _____

Check your answers on page 96.

Compound Verbs

When two verbs apply to the same subject, they can be joined by the conjunctions *and, but,* or *or,* forming a **compound verb**.

   <u>Vivian</u> <u>read and reread</u> the bus schedule.

In this example Vivian (the subject) performed two actions. She <u>read</u>, and she <u>reread</u>.

Often a compound verb is split by other phrases. A helping verb can apply to both main verbs, however. You may repeat the helping verb to add emphasis to the second verb if you like.

Correct: Vivian <u>has picked</u> up her handbag *and* <u>grabbed</u> her coat.

Correct: Vivian <u>has picked</u> up her handbag *and* <u>has grabbed</u> her coat.

The words *up her handbag* separate the compound verb. In the first sentence the helping verb, *has,* applies to both main verbs, *picked* and *grabbed.* In the second sentence the helping verb is repeated. This slows the sentence and emphasizes the two separate actions.

The conjunctions *or* and *but* can be used to contrast two actions.

She <u>will run</u> to the corner *or* <u>miss</u> the bus.

She <u>ran</u> to the corner *but* <u>missed</u> the bus.

In the first sentence *or* contrasts the subject's choices: Either she will have to run, *or* she will miss the bus. In the second sentence *but* contrasts the subject's effort with the outcome: She ran, *but* she missed the bus anyway.

In any case, each verb must match the subject as singular or plural.

Incorrect: Vivian and Shyrone <u>walks</u> to the bus stop and <u>waits</u>.

Correct: Vivian and Shyrone <u>walk</u> to the bus stop and <u>wait</u>.

Since the subject (Vivian and Shyrone) is plural, the verbs must be plural, too. <u>They</u> <u>walk</u> and <u>wait</u>. The phrase *to the bus stop* separates the two verbs, but both verbs are performed by the same plural subject.

Exercise 3.2

Choose a conjunction (*and, but,* or *or*) and complete each sentence. Write the whole new sentence including a second verb and a thought completer, if necessary. Be sure the new verb refers to the original subject. Underline the subject once and the verbs twice. Try to use each conjunction at least once. An example is done for you.

Example: Emery was sitting in the front of the bus (*and, but, or*)
<u>Emery</u> was sitting in the front of the bus but <u>gave</u> his seat to an elderly woman.

1. The brakes of the truck behind them squealed (*and, but, or*)

and stopped.

_____

_____

2. The passengers all looked back *(and, but, or)*

_____ *and tailed.*

_____

3. The truck might stop in time *(and, but, or)*

_____ *or go through the traffic light.*

_____

4. Emery bumped into the elderly woman *(and, but, or)*

_____ *and hurted.*

_____

5. The elderly woman groaned *(and, but, or)* ‏סיפר נ.ע

_____ *but wasn't wounded.*

_____

Check your answers on page 97.

Using Three or More Subjects or Verbs

Lesson 3

When you use three or more subjects or verbs, write the conjunction *and* or *or* before the last item. You may also use the conjunction pairs *either . . . or* and *neither . . . nor*. In all cases, separate the items with a comma, and place a comma before the conjunction.

When you check your writing, look for any series of items. If you have only two items, then do *not* use a comma. If you have three or more items, you should have one fewer comma than items. This rule holds true for all series: nouns, verbs, adjectives, or adverbs.

Emery, Vivian, *and* Shyrone rode to work together.

The three elements of the compound subject are separated by commas and by *and*. There are three items and two commas.

Vivian *neither* planned, prepared, served, *nor* cleaned up dinner.

The conjunction pair *neither . . . nor* connects the four elements of this compound verb. There are four items and three commas.

Read each sentence. On the line below each sentence, copy the compound subjects or verbs adding the correct punctuation if needed. An example is done for you.

Example: Men women and children were riding the bus.
<u>Men, women, and children</u>

1. The driver sped, failed to signal, and ran a red light.

   _____

2. The police chased and pulled over the bus.

   _____

3. The driver shouted, cursed, and left the bus.

   _____

4. Neither Ned nor Rick thought she was drunk.

   _____

5. Reporters, pedestrians, and police officers crowded around the scene.

   _____

Check your answers on page 97.

Lesson 4
Writing Compound Sentences

A **compound sentence** is made of two or more independent clauses joined by a conjunction (*and, but,* or *or*). Each clause could stand as a separate sentence. Together, however, the clauses complete a larger thought.

Two Simple Sentences:	The taxi licensing test was hard. Emery knew the material.
One Compound Sentence:	The taxi licensing test was hard, *but* Emery knew the material.

The two simple sentences are related, but we don't see exactly how. The compound sentence uses the conjunction *but* to contrast the two ideas. Even though it was a hard test, Emery was ready for it.

A comma is used to separate clauses in a compound sentence. The comma is placed before the conjunction.

Exercise 3.4

Read each numbered item. Then choose a clause from the list below to form a compound sentence. Mark the clause so you don't use it twice. Use a conjunction to write the compound sentence in the space provided. An example is done for you.

Example: The 20-trip fare card cost $40.
        The 20-trip fare card cost $40, but Shyrone only had $25.

1. The ten-trip fare card cost $22.50.

   _____, and _____

   _____

2. To get to work, she took the N2 bus.

   _____, and then _____

   _____

3. The whole trip took 45 minutes.

   _____, but _____

   _____

4. She could keep taking the bus to work.

   _____, or _____

   _____

5. The train was faster.

   _____, but _____

   _____

Clauses to Complete the Sentences Above

   __5__   It was more expensive.
   __1__   Shyrone bought one.
   __x__   Shyrone only had $25.
   __3__   The time passed quickly.
   __2__   Then she transferred to the AA bus.
   __4__   She could start taking the train.

Check your answers on page 97.

Fixing Run-on Sentences

A **run-on sentence** contains two or more complete thoughts that are not clearly related, separated, or connected.

SENTENCES THAT RUN TOGETHER

Some run-on sentences are thoughts that are run together. The reader is not sure where one idea ends and another begins.

Incorrect: The timetable listed all the trains arriving at the station on time was important.

This example is confusing because we first think *the trains arriving at the station* is a phrase. As we read, however, we realize that *arriving at the station on time was important* is a separate thought.

One solution is to break apart this run-on sentence.

Correct: The timetable listed all the trains. Arriving at the station on time was important.

A problem still remains, though. We are not quite sure *whose* arriving on time is important. The second sentence could be rewritten.

Rewritten: The timetable listed all the trains. Now we knew when to arrive at the station.

FIXING COMMA SPLICES

A comma may not join independent clauses. A comma used in this way is called a comma splice. This incorrect usage can be fixed in a number of ways.

Incorrect: Vivian didn't want the M15 bus, she wanted the N12.

One correction of the comma splice is to simply start a new sentence at the comma.

Correct: Vivian didn't want the M15 bus. She wanted the N12.

You can also replace the comma splice with a **semicolon** (;). This is acceptable when the ideas in the two clauses are very clearly related.

Correct: Vivian didn't want the M15 bus; she wanted the N12.

A third way to correct a comma splice is to create a compound sentence.

Correct: Vivian didn't want the M15 bus, but she wanted the N12.

Exercise 3.5

Read the following run-on sentences. Rewrite them correctly in the space provided. You may use four "correction strategies": (a) form separate sentences, (b) rewrite as two sentences, (c) create compound sentences, and (d) use semicolons. Try to use each of these strategies at least once. An example is done for you.

Example: The train station was filled with weary people waiting at the end of a workday is exhausting.
The train station was filled with weary people. Waiting at the end of a workday is exhausting.

1. The city transportation department has a telephone line to help people using a complex system of buses and trains can be confusing.

   _____

   _____

2. Vivian took the bus she preferred the train.   (, but/yet)

   Vivian took the bus; however, she preferred the train.

   _____

3. The man didn't buy a ticket, he jumped over the entrance barrier and boarded the train.

   The man didn't buy a tricket; he jumped over the entrance

   _____

4. She didn't get off at the library, she went all the way to Elmer Avenue.

   _____

   _____

5. The driver looked at the rear axle, a mechanic examined the engine.

   The driver looked at the rear axle, and a mechanic examined the engine.

Check your answers on page 97.

axle

Building Your Word Power

In your word notebook include the Key Terms and Life Skill Words from this chapter. Break each word into syllables or into word parts (prefixes, suffixes, and roots). Write an original sentence for at least five of the words.

Building Your Writing Power: Ask Questions

One way to think of things to write is to ask questions about a topic. Use the question words *who, what, when, where, how,* and *why* to help get your thoughts moving.

If your topic was *taxi cabs*, for instance, you might write these questions:

Who rides in cabs?

What is the difference between "medallion" cabs and "gypsy" cabs?

When was the last time I rode in a cab?

Assignment: Choose a topic of your own, and write at least five questions about it. If two of your questions are related, try rewriting them as one compound question.

Building Your Editing Checklist

Add the following items to the editing checklist that you began in Chapter 2:

- Use a conjunction *(and, or)* to form a compound subject when the verb applies to each individual subject.
- Use a conjunction *(and, but, or)* to form a compound verb when the subject performs each action.
- Use commas and a conjunction to list a series of three or more elements in a compound subject or verb.
- Use a comma and a conjunction *(and, but, or)* to join independent clauses into a compound sentence.
- Fix run-on sentences by (a) forming separate sentences, (b) rewriting sentences, (c) creating compound sentences, and (d) using semicolons.

Use your editing checklist to improve the sentences in your portfolio.

Chapter 4

Subject-Verb Agreement

"Well, Aunt Matty left you the family bible, Sis," Michael Derby repeated patiently into the telephone.

"I heard you, but I don't understand. She lived with you and Dad. I live way out here and I hardly ever visit," said Michael's sister Darlene, sounding a little guilty.

"Look, it's OK. She wanted you to have it. I'll mail it to you," Michael reassured her.

"Maybe you should hold it until I come again. It might get lost or damaged," Darlene protested.

"You spent your last dime coming for the funeral. You might as well have the bible now. I know how to wrap and address a package. Don't worry!" Michael continued, "I'll send it **certified mail** or **registered mail**, or whatever they call it. That way the package will be numbered and the post office can **trace** it, just in case. And I'll pay extra for a **return receipt**. You'll have to sign for it, and I'll get a postcard after you get the package."

"What if they damage it?"

"I'll wrap it in padding, and I'll **insure** it for $500, too," Michael sighed.

"Be sure to wrap it carefully. And don't forget your **return address**," Darlene lectured.

"You know, you sound more and more like Aunt Matty every day!" Michael laughed.

Key Terms

- singular
- subject-verb agreement
- verb phrase
- plural

Life Skill Words

- certified mail
- commemorative stamp
- insured mail
- issue
- postal service
- registered mail
- return address
- return receipt
- trace

Subject-Verb Agreement with Regular Verbs

As you learned in Chapter 1 a *subject* tells what or who a sentence is about. A *verb* helps make a statement about a subject.

Subject-verb agreement means that subjects and verbs must match in *number*. A **singular** subject stands for only one person, place, or thing. The verb that tells about a singular subject must be in the singular form. A **plural** subject represents more than one person, place, or thing. Likewise, a verb that tells about a plural subject must be written in the plural form.

Incorrect:	Michael walk to the post office.
Correct:	Michael <u>walks</u> to the post office.

The subject, *Michael,* is singular. The singular form of the verb *to walk* is *walks.*

Incorrect:	I puts on the stamps after you addresses the package.
Correct:	<u>I</u> <u>put</u> on the stamps after <u>you</u> <u>address</u> the package.

The subjects, *I* and *you,* take verbs without *-s* or *-es* endings.

To decide which verb form matches a subject, you can replace the noun subject with a pronoun in your mind. Notice that the verb form stays the same when the subject changes from noun to pronoun.

Noun Subjects	Pronoun Subjects	Number
<u>Michael</u> <u>buys</u> stamps.	<u>He</u> <u>buys</u> stamps.	singular
<u>Darlene</u> <u>wraps</u> packages.	<u>She</u> <u>wraps</u> packages.	singular
The <u>package</u> <u>weighs</u> a pound.	<u>It</u> <u>weighs</u> a pound.	singular
	<u>I</u> <u>sign</u> the receipt.	singular
	<u>You</u> <u>open</u> the letter.	singular
<u>Michael and I</u> <u>send</u> a gift.	<u>We</u> <u>send</u> a gift.	plural
<u>You and Michael</u> <u>play</u> music.	<u>You</u> <u>play</u> music.	plural
<u>David and Michael</u> <u>ride</u> home.	<u>They</u> <u>ride</u> home.	plural

RULES FOR REGULAR PRESENT TENSE VERBS

Singular verbs that follow *he, she,* and *it* have *-s* or *-es* endings.
Singular verbs that follow *I* and *you* have no endings.
Plural verbs have no endings.

Exercise 4.1a

In each sentence underline the subject once. Then underline the proper form of the verb twice. An example is done for you.

Example: <u>Michael</u> (pick / <u>picks</u>) up the mail on the way home from work.

1. The Derbys (get / gets) a few sympathy cards each day.
2. Sally (shop / shops) for flowers.
3. They (smell / smells) fresh.
4. Michael (miss / misses) his aunt.
5. The easy chair (remind / reminds) him of her.
6. Now you (cook / cooks) dinner by yourself.
7. Michael and his father (eat / eats) together most evenings.
8. I (write / writes) to Darlene once a week.
9. The package (arrive / arrives) early in the day.
10. It (touch / touches) Darlene's heart.

Check your answers on page 97.

Exercise 4.1b

Mark the six sentences from Exercise 4.1a that have noun subjects. Rewrite these sentences in the spaces provided using *pronoun* subjects. Underline the subject once and the verb twice. An example is done for you.

Example: <u>He</u> <u>picks</u> up the mail on the way home from work.

_____

_____

_____

_____

_____

_____

Check your answers on page 97.

Lesson 2

The Verbs "To Be" and "To Have"

The verbs *to be* and *to have* follow their own patterns that depend on the subject pronoun and the tense of the sentence. You have to memorize the forms of *irregular verbs* such as these.

THE VERB *TO BE*

One of the most commonly used verbs is *to be*. Its present and past tense forms are shown below.

PRESENT AND PAST TENSES OF THE VERB *TO BE*

Subject	Present Tense	Past Tense
I	am	was
we, you, they	are	were
he, she, it	is	was

The verb *to be* is also used as a *helping verb* to form *progressive* tenses. The helping verb and the main verb make up a **verb phrase**. The helping verb agrees with the subject. The main verb stays the same.

Present:	I <u>am</u> her nephew.
Past:	She <u>was</u> my favorite aunt.
Present Progressive:	We <u>are going</u> to miss her.
	I <u>am going</u> to miss her.
	She <u>is going</u> to miss her.

Notice the verb phrases in the last three examples. The helping verbs *(are, am, is)* change to agree with the subject, but the main verb *(going)* stays the same.

THE VERB *TO HAVE*

Like *to be*, the verb *to have* can be used in the present and past tenses. It can also be used as a helping verb to form *perfect* tenses. Again, in verb phrases helping verbs must agree with the subject, and main verbs stay the same.

PRESENT TENSE OF THE VERB *TO HAVE*

Subject	Verb Form
I, You, We, They	have
He, She, It	has

The past tense of *to have* is *had* for all subjects.

Present:	You <u>have</u> my sympathy.
Past:	She <u>had</u> a warm smile.
Present Perfect:	We <u>have gone</u> to church.
	I <u>have gone</u> to the bakery.
	She <u>has gone</u> to a better place.

Notice that in the last three examples the verb *to have* agrees with the subject. The main verb *(gone)* does not change.

Exercise 4.2

Write a sentence using each subject with the correct form and tense of the verb shown in parentheses. Underline the subject once and the verb or verb phrase twice. An example is done for you.

Example: Present tense: I *(to be)* . . .

<u>I</u> <u>am</u> free for the day.

1. Past tense: You *(to have)* . . .

2. Present tense: Robert *(to have)* . . .

3. Present progressive tense: They *(to be)* waiting . . .

4. Present perfect tense: We *(to have)* sold . . .

5. Present tense: I *(to be)* . . .

6. Past tense: You *(to be)* . . .

7. Present tense: Susan *(to have)* . . .

8. Present progressive tense: It *(to be)* standing . . .

_____

9. Present perfect tense: She *(to have)* left . . .

_____

10. Present tense: I *(to have)* . . .

_____

Check your answers on page 97.

Compound Subjects

As you learned in Chapter 3, nouns or pronouns can be joined by conjunctions to form compound subjects. When the conjunction *and* joins subject elements, the subject is plural.

> Michael and his father walk every evening.
> They walk every evening.

The compound subject *Michael and his father* can be replaced by the plural pronoun *They*.

When the conjunction *or* joins subject elements, however, the verb agrees with the last subject element.

> Michael or his daughters shop on Saturdays.
> His daughters or Michael shops on Saturdays.

We are not really sure who does the shopping, so the verb *to shop* agrees with the last subject element.

Several conjunction pairs work like *or: either/or, neither/nor, not only/but also*.

> *Either* the package *or* the stamps are lost.
> *Neither* the stamps *nor* the package is lost.
> *Not only* the stamps *but also* the package is lost.

As with compound subjects joined with *or*, the verb agrees with the last subject element.

In each sentence underline the compound subject once. Then underline the proper form of the verb twice. An example is done for you.

Example: <u>Michael and his father</u> (<u>walk</u> / walks) to the post office.

1. Neither he nor his father (need / needs) the exercise.
2. Either the package or the letters (are / is) waiting for them.
3. Neither the letter carrier nor her note (have / has) said for sure.
4. Not only the men but also the girls (were / was) anxious for the delivery.
5. Mary and Jill (wait / waits) impatiently at home.

Check your answers on page 98.

Finding the Subject Far from its Verb

Sometimes a phrase comes between a subject and verb. It might describe the subject. It might add useful, but nonessential, information. In either case, the interrupting phrase does not change the agreement between the subject and verb.

The <u>bag</u> of letters <u>hangs</u> from her shoulder.

The bag (singular) hangs. The phrase *of letters* tells what kind of bag.

The <u>letters</u> in the box <u>contain</u> important information.

The letters (plural) contain the information. The phrase *in the box* tells which letters.

The <u>supervisor</u>, as well as the clerks, <u>was looking</u> for the letter.

The supervisor is the singular subject. The verb *was looking* agrees with it. The phrase *as well as the clerks* is a nonessential detail set off by commas. The sentence is about the supervisor.

To find the subject of a sentence, you must decide *who* or *what* the sentence is about.

Exercise 4.4

In each sentence underline the subject once. Then underline the proper form of the verb or helping verb twice. Cross out any interrupting or nonessential phrase between the subject and verb. An example is done for you.

Example: Stamps ~~with an attractive design~~ (<u>attract</u> / attracts) attention.

1. This sheet of stamps (contain / contains) five sets of four wildflowers.
2. The publication of a new stamp design (are / is) called an **issue**.
3. The subjects of a **commemorative** issue (are / is) being honored.
4. Heroes of the Civil War (were / was) honored by a recent commemorative stamp.
5. Several inventors, as well as one scientist, (were / was) featured on a series of stamps.

Check your answers on page 98.

The Subject of Sentences that Begin with "There"

There is not the subject of a sentence, even if it begins a sentence. The subject is the noun or pronoun *after* the verb. *There* is a warning that the subject is later in the sentence. The verb, of course, must agree with the subject.

There <u>are</u> many <u>products</u> <u>offered</u> by the **postal service**.
Products is the subject, and *are offered* is its plural verb.

There <u>is</u> a <u>variety</u> of services <u>offered</u>, as well.
Variety is the subject, and *is offered* is its singular verb.

Most sentences that begin with *there* can be rewritten more clearly.

Many <u>products</u> <u>are offered</u> by the postal service.
A <u>variety</u> of services <u>is offered</u>, as well.

Notice that these rewrites make the subject clearer. The subjects *products* and *variety* are not performing any action, however.

You can change the focus of these sentences by rewriting them using active subjects and verbs.

The postal <u>service</u> <u>offers</u> many products.
<u>It</u> <u>offers</u> a variety of services, as well.

Here, the subjects and verbs are active. The *service offers. It offers.*

You can combine these ideas into one sentence.

The postal <u>service</u> <u>offers</u> a variety of products and services.

When you identify your subject and verb, you can be sure they agree in number. You can also be sure you are stating your ideas clearly and strongly.

Exercise 4.5

In each sentence underline the subject once. Then underline the proper form of the verb twice. Then rewrite the sentence putting the subject before the verb. You may use a different verb to make the sentence clearer or stronger. An example is done for you.

Example: There (<u>are</u> / is) many <u>people</u> in line in the post office.
<u>Many people are standing in line in the post office.</u>

1. There (are / is) only one clerk behind the counter.

   _____

2. There (are / is) a woman tapping her foot impatiently.

   _____

3. There (are / is) two little boys leaning on the display case.

   _____

4. There (are / is) a friendly customer chatting with the clerk.

   _____

5. There (are / is) several people fidgeting and mumbling in line.

   _____

Check your answers on page 98.

Building Your Word Power

In your word notebook include the Key Terms and Life Skill Words from this chapter. Break each word into syllables or into word parts (prefixes, suffixes, and roots). Write an original sentence for at least five of the words.

Building Your Writing Power: Answering Questions

In Chapter 3 you wrote questions about a topic in order to develop ideas for writing. The answers to these questions can come from several places. For answers that are a matter of your own opinion, just write down your ideas. Other answers may come from:

- Friends and family
- Experts
- Books and magazines

When you seek these answers you are conducting *research*. Take notes, and expect to ask additional questions as you learn more about your subject.

Assignment: Return to the questions you wrote at the end of Chapter 3. Answer at least three of these questions with information you gather from other people or from books or magazines. You may want to take notes and then write your answers in complete sentences.

Be sure to save your work in your portfolio.

Building Your Editing Checklist

Add the following items to the editing checklist that you began in Chapter 2:

- Check that verbs match subjects in *number.*
- Check forms of the verb *to be* and *to have.*
- Use a plural verb for compound subjects joined with *and.*
- Make the verb agree with the last element of a compound subject joined with *or.*
- Identify the subject of each sentence. Recognize interrupting phrases.
- Identify the subjects of sentences beginning with *There.* Rewrite these sentences if they are awkward.

Chapter 5

Verb Agreement with Indefinite Pronouns and Collective Nouns

"Would you like to go to the movies some time?" Robert Jong asked casually.

Li Hua could feel her palms perspire, but she managed to sound confident. "Sure, Bob, I'd like that. I'll need to get a babysitter, though."

"We could take Chong along, if you like," Bob offered.

"Well, he's only nine. What do you think we could all see?" Li Hua wondered.

"I'll buy a newspaper. Let's check the **movie listings** at lunch time," Bob suggested.

"OK, it's a date—for lunch, that is," Li Hua smiled.

In the cafeteria Bob was checking the **ratings** of the movies now playing in their neighborhood. The films he liked were all rated **PG-13** or **R**, and he was sure Li Hua wouldn't want Chong to see them. He read the **reviews** of the movies rated **G** and **PG**. They seemed a bit dull. Maybe inviting the kid along was a mistake.

"I guess I'll have to decide which I want more, a date with Li Hua or a good movie!" Bob chuckled to himself.

Key Terms

- antecedent
- collective noun
- indefinite pronoun

Life Skill Words

- box office
- G rating
- movie listing
- movie ratings
- movie review
- PG rating
- PG-13 rating
- R rating

Singular Indefinite Pronouns

As you know, a pronoun stands for a noun—a person, place, thing, idea, or emotion. The noun that a pronoun stands for is called its **antecedent**.

> Bob asked *Li Hua* to go to a movie. *She* was pleased.
>
> *She* is a pronoun standing for the antecedent noun *Li Hua*.

An **indefinite pronoun** also stands for a noun, but does not identify its antecedent specifically. The words *another, each, every, either, neither, much,* and *one* are always considered singular when they are used as pronouns.

> We expected to see two movies, but we got there late. <u>One</u> <u>was</u> just ending, and <u>another</u> <u>was</u> about to begin.

In the example, the words *one* and *another* stand for movies, but we are not sure which ones. These indefinite pronouns are used as singular subjects.

> "Let's see the horror movies, *Chain Saw Party* and *Electric Nightmare*."
>
> "<u>Either</u> <u>sounds</u> awful. <u>Neither</u> <u>suits</u> my taste."

In the example, the words *either* and *neither* refer to one of the horror movies. Again, these pronouns are indefinite because they do not identify their antecedent exactly. They are used as singular subjects. Their verbs, *sounds* and *suits,* are in the singular form.

Exercise 5.1

Complete each sentence using the correct form of the verb in parentheses. Underline the subject once and the verb twice. An example is done for you.

Example: Another (*to be:* present tense) walking down the aisle.

<u>Another</u> <u>is</u> walking down the aisle.

1. Each (*to be:* past tense) reviewed by a newspaper.

2. Neither (*to have:* present tense) started on time.

3. Much (*to be:* past tense) said about this film.

_____

4. One (*to play:* present tense) all day and night.

_____

5. Another (*to sound:* present tense) good to me.

_____

Check your answers on page 98.

Interrupting Phrases

Indefinite pronouns are sometimes used with phrases that come before the verb. These interrupting phrases do not change the form of the verb. A singular pronoun takes a singular verb.

Incorrect:	One of the boys buy popcorn.
Correct:	<u>One</u> of the boys <u>buys</u> popcorn.

The correct subject-verb is *one buys* (not *boys buy*).

Incorrect:	Either of the movies' titles scare me.
Correct:	<u>Either</u> of the movies' titles <u>scares</u> me.

The correct subject-verb is *either scares* (not *titles scare*).

_____

Exercise 5.2

In each sentence underline the subject once. Then underline the proper form of the verb twice. An example is done for you.

Example: <u>Each</u> of these R-rated films (<u>contain</u> / contains) violence.

1. Another of those scenes (have / has) me on the edge of my seat.
2. Every one of the actors (is / are) so handsome.
3. Much of these movies (was / were) devoted to car chases.

4. Neither of those people (are / is) keeping quiet.

5. Each of those **G-rated** cartoons (pleases / please) children.

Check your answers on page 98.

Plural Indefinite Pronouns

Some indefinite pronouns are *always* plural. Others may be singular or plural, depending on how they are used.

INDEFINITE PRONOUNS THAT ARE ALWAYS PLURAL

The following indefinite pronouns are always plural: *both, few, many,* and *several.*

> Both have happy endings.
> Many are called, but few are chosen.

In the examples, *both, many,* and *few* are used as plural subjects. Their verbs take the plural form: *have, are called, are chosen.*

The words *both, few, many,* and *several* can also be used as adjectives. The nouns they describe are always plural.

> Both movies have happy endings.
> Many listeners are called, but few lucky people are chosen as winners.

In the examples, *both* describes *movies, many* describes *listeners,* and *few* describes *people. Movies, listeners,* and *people* are plural nouns acting as subjects of their clauses. The verbs are plural.

INDEFINITE PRONOUNS THAT MAY BE SINGULAR OR PLURAL

The following indefinite pronouns may be singular or plural, depending on the noun that they refer to: *all, none, any, some, more,* and *most.* Often, a noun follows these pronouns in a phrase beginning with *of: all of my children, none of the seats,* and so on.

> Some of the children were interested in the **R-rated** movie.
> Some of the candy costs too much.

In the first example, *some* refers to the plural *children* and takes the plural verb *were.* In the second example, *some* refers to the singular *candy* and takes the singular verb *costs.*

In each sentence underline the indefinite pronoun subject once. Then draw an arrow to the noun that it refers to. Finally, underline the proper form of the verb twice. An example is done for you.

Example: <u>All</u> the people (<u>have</u> / has) been seated.

1. More than one customer (has / have) walked out.

2. Most of the popcorn (are / is) buttered.

3. Most of the posters (is / are) above eye level.

4. None of the theater (are / is) quiet.

5. None of the actors (are / is) talented.

6. More of the scenes (has / have) "adult situations."

7. Some of the coming attractions (look / looks) interesting.

8. All of the soda (is / are) gone.

9. Some of the people (has / have) fallen asleep.

10. Any of the ushers (look / looks) bored.

Check your answers on page 98.

Verb Agreement with Indefinite Pronouns

Always Singular

another, each, every, either, neither, much, one

Always Plural

both, few, many, several

Singular or Plural, Depending on the Noun Referred to

all, any, more, most, none, some

Read the following sentences. All have indefinite pronouns as subjects. In each sentence underline the subject once. Refer to the *Verb Agreement with Indefinite Pronouns* table on page 44. Then underline the proper form of the verb twice. An example is done for you.

Example: <u>Another</u> of those advertisements (come / <u>comes</u>) on now.

1. Few (holds / hold) my attention like that one.
2. None of these films (is / are) worth seeing.
3. Each of the movies (was / were) a hit.
4. More of the **box offices** (sell / sells) reserved seats now.
5. Any of those nude scenes (makes / make) the film R-rated.
6. Some of that strong language (bother / bothers) me.
7. One of my favorite stars (has / have) retired in poor health.
8. Several in this film (have / has) been seen on TV.
9. Either of those seats (is / are) good enough.
10. Most of my friends (talks / talk) about movies.

Check your answers on page 99.

Lesson 4

Collective Nouns

A **collective noun** represents a group of people, animals, or things. Generally, you should use singular verbs and pronouns with collective nouns. Sometimes, however, collective nouns are used as plurals.

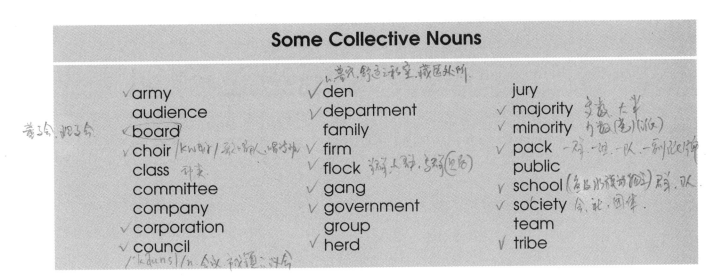

Some Collective Nouns

army	den	jury
audience	department	majority
board	family	minority
choir	firm	pack
class	flock	public
committee	gang	school
company	government	society
corporation	group	team
council	herd	tribe

COLLECTIVE NOUNS STANDING FOR SINGULAR UNITS

When you think of the group acting as a unit, treat the collective noun as singular. Use the singular form of verbs and pronouns.

> The bowling <u>league</u> <u>meets</u> on Wednesdays.
> The <u>herd</u> <u>crosses</u> the river.

Each of these subjects acts as a single group.

> The <u>school board</u> <u>has agreed</u> to present its budget next week.

Although the board has several members, in this example it is acting as a single unit. It takes the singular verb *has*. Notice that the pronoun *its* is also singular to agree with *school board*.

COLLECTIVE NOUNS STANDING FOR PLURAL MEMBERS

When you think of the members of a group acting separately, treat the collective noun as plural. Use the plural form of verbs and pronouns.

> *Awkward:*   The <u>council</u> <u>have</u> not decided what action *they* should take.

Here we imagine the individual members discussing their options. *Council* takes the plural verb *have* and the plural pronoun *they*. Plural uses of collective nouns can sound awkward, however. You can rewrite the sentence to change the subject to the *members* of the council.

> *Improved:*   The <u>members</u> of the council <u>have</u> not decided what action *they* should take.

To be clear, use the name for the elements in the group when they act separately.

> *Awkward:*   The <u>pack</u> <u>scatter</u> at the sound of gunshots.
> *Improved:*   The <u>wolves</u> in the pack <u>scatter</u> at the sound of gunshots.
> *Or:*   The <u>wolves</u> <u>scatter</u> at the sound of gunshots.

Sometimes, as in the last example, the collective noun is not essential. The pack can be replaced by the individual wolves who scatter.

The subject and verb are the core of any clause. Your reader should know instantly who is doing what or what is being described. Making subjects and verbs agree helps the reader understand your meaning.

Exercise 5.4

The subjects of the following sentences are collective nouns. Underline each subject once. Decide if the subject is acting as a singular unit or as separate members. Then underline the correct form of the verb twice. Rewrite awkward plural uses in the space provided. An example is done for you.

Example: The <u>police force</u> (<u>argue</u> / argues) over shift assignments.
<u>Members of the police force argue over shift assignments.</u>

1. The movie club (meet / meets) once a month.

   _____

2. The choir (are / is) fighting over solo selections.

   _____

3. The cub scout den (have / has) worked hard for their merit badges.

   _____

   _____

4. The government (are / is) cutting taxes and services.

   _____

5. The jury (have / has) argued over the evidence for two days.

   _____

   _____

6. An army (move / moves) on its stomach.

   _____

7. The committee (were / was) debating the plan.

   _____

8. The flock (land / lands) on the lake like a single bird.

   _____

9. The football team (were / was) struggling with their homework.

_____

_____

10. The company (are / is) going to open another store.

_____

Check your answers on page 99.

Writing Assignments

Reading to Write

Clip or photocopy a review of a current movie from a newspaper or magazine. Then do the following:

- Write one or two sentences explaining why the movie was rated G, PG, PG-13, R, or NC-17.
- Decide if you would recommend the film to a friend. Write two or three sentences explaining your opinion.

Save your work in your portfolio.

Building Your Editing Checklist

Add the following items to the editing checklist that you began in Chapter 2:

- When you use an indefinite pronoun as a subject, use a verb that agrees in number:

  Always singular: another, each, every, either, neither, much, one

  Always plural: both, few, many, several

  Depends on noun: all, any, more, most, none, some

- Generally, treat collective nouns (words that refer to groups) as singular.
- When members of a group are divided, treat the collective noun as plural.
- Consider rewriting sentences where collective nouns are divided.

Chapter 6

Complex Sentences with Adjective Clauses

Sergio DiPalma thought of his boyhood in Italy. That was a long time ago, and young boys got in trouble then, too. Here in the library, Sergio had the quiet to think about his son, Salvatore, and about his grandson, Nicholas.

"Pop, I don't know what to do," Sal had told him, "Nicky is hanging out with a tough crowd."

Sergio had listened patiently.

"Gina says I should spend more time with him. Maybe get him into the youth group at St. Agnes," his son continued. "Maybe I should volunteer to work with the kids there. I just don't know what I would do with them."

Sergio agreed to help. He asked at the **reference desk** about activities for teenaged boys. Mark Jefferson, the librarian, suggested a book about organizing boys clubs. He also said they could get a **training video** through the **interlibrary loan** program. A **catalog** listed the titles and descriptions of materials available. The materials he could order were free and would arrive in a week.

"I see some movies the boys would like, too," Sergio nodded, "And the church has a VCR. I will tell my son."

Key Terms

- adjective clause
- complex sentence
- essential clause
- main clause
- nonessential clause
- relative pronoun

Life Skill Words

- card catalog
- catalog
- drama
- fiction   *story but not true*
- interlibrary loan
- reference desk
- science fiction
- stagecraft
- training video

nonfiction true

Matrix

Adjective Clauses

As you learned in Chapter 2, a *dependent clause* contains a subject and a verb, but it does not express a complete thought. A sentence that includes a dependent clause is called a **complex sentence**. A **main clause**, or *independent clause*, is the heart of a complex sentence. A dependent clause often modifies, or tells about, part of the main clause.

When a clause modifies a noun or pronoun, it is an **adjective clause**. Adjective clauses answer the questions *What kind? Which one?* or *How many?*

main clause   adjective clause
Sergio <u>was carrying</u> a book (<u>that told</u> about youth groups).

In the example, the main clause is *Sergio was carrying a book.* The dependent clause (in parentheses) is *that told about youth groups.* It acts as an adjective telling *what kind* of book.

An adjective clause is introduced by a **relative pronoun**: *who, whom, which,* or *that.* These words introduce more information about a noun or pronoun. The pronoun *who, that,* or *which* often acts as subject of the adjective clause. In the example above, *that* is the subject of the adjective clause and refers to *book.*

Sometimes an adjective clause comes between the subject and verb of the main clause.

―――― adjective clause―――――
subject (subject   verb)   verb
The <u>book,</u> (<u>which came</u> from the library), <u>gave</u> information about organization and activities.

Here the adjective clause comes between the subject and verb of the main clause, *book* and *gave.* The subject of the dependent clause (in parentheses) is *which,* and its verb is *came.*

The relative pronouns *that* and *which* are used to refer to places, animals, and things. Use *who* to refer to people.

―――― adjective clause―――――
subject   (subject verb)   verb
Mr. <u>Jefferson,</u> (<u>who   is</u> our reference librarian), <u>recommended</u> a film on popular dance and several dance music recordings.

Here, *who* is the subject of the adjective clause and refers to a person, *Mr. Jefferson.*

(anything, something + that 以 w)

不能用 which)

先行词语，

In each clause, underline the subject once and the verb twice. Put the adjective clause in parentheses. Then draw an arrow from the relative pronoun to the word it stands for. An example is done for you.

非限制性定语从句，力能用 that

Example: The <u>music</u>, (<u>which</u> <u>was</u> fun to dance to), <u>was</u> popular forty
years ago.

1. The <u>tapes</u> (<u>that</u> <u>were borrowed</u>) <u>sounded</u> modern.

2. Gina, who was Nick's mother, looked into the recreation hall.

3. The hall, which was converted from an old hardware store, belonged to the church.   多余，限制句.

4. Sal watched the video that coached youth center volunteers.

5. The <u>video</u> <u>focused</u> on the theme of respect, which is the key to a successful social organization.

Check your answers on page 99.

Adjective Clauses with Independent Subjects

Lesson 2

In an adjective clause the relative pronoun does not always act as the subject. The relative pronoun still refers to a noun in the main clause but the subject of the dependent clause is independent of the main clause. These clauses are introduced by *whom, that,* and *which.*

The <u>suggestion</u> (*that* <u>we</u> <u>sponsor</u> a comic book signing) <u>came</u> from Nicholas.

The adjective clause tells which suggestion came from Nicholas. Its subject is *we,* and its verb is *sponsor.* The relative pronoun *that* replaces *suggestion* in the dependent clause.

that 在从句中作宾语可省略.

Use *whom* to refer to a pronoun that is an object in the adjective clause.

The <u>illustrator</u> (*whom* <u>Nick</u> <u>admired</u>) <u>signed</u> Nick's copy of her latest comic book.

The adjective clause identifies the illustrator. The word *whom* refers to this person. It is used as an object—the person *<u>Nick</u> <u>admired</u>*.

Exercise 6.2

In each clause underline the subject once and the verb twice. Put the adjective clause in parentheses. Then draw an arrow from the relative pronoun to the word it stands for. An example is done for you.

Example: The homework <u>center</u> (that <u>Sal</u> <u>started</u>) <u>took</u> a lot of work on his part.

1. He checked with teachers at the school (that most of the kids <u>attended</u>.)

2. At the library, <u>Sal</u> <u>searched</u> for materials in the **card catalog,** (which Mr. Jefferson <u>explained</u> to him.)

3. <u>Mr. Jefferson</u> (whom <u>Sal</u> <u>respected,</u>) <u>recommended</u> several high-interest books of **fiction** for the youth group's library.

4. <u>Sal</u> <u>convinced</u> Nick to organize the group's **science fiction** comic books, (which many <u>members</u> <u>had read</u> and <u>scattered.</u>)

5. <u>Sal</u> <u>worked</u> with Father Joseph, (whom <u>Sal</u> <u>trusted.</u>)

Check your answers on page 100.

Essential and Nonessential Adjective Clauses

Lesson 3

An **essential clause** provides information needed to make the sentence meaningful. Without that clause the main clause would change or seem incomplete. Essential clauses are *not* set off by commas.

The <u>videotape</u> <u>teaches</u> dances (<u>that</u> <u>are</u> fun to learn).

This sentence focuses on what kind of dances the videotape teaches. The adjective clause provides that essential information: dances *that are fun to learn.*

A **nonessential clause** provides extra information. Without this information the meaning of the sentence would still be complete. Nonessential clauses are set off by commas.

The <u>dances</u>, (<u>which</u> <u>are</u> fun to learn), <u>are taught</u> by videotape.

This sentence focuses on how the dances are taught—by videotape. The adjective clause provides extra information about the dances.

An adjective clause is essential when it specifically identifies an element of the main clause that would otherwise have been unclear. When the element described is already clearly identified, it is nonessential.

Essential:	The person *who used to run the youth group* now works for a school across town.
Nonessential:	Mr. Greco, *who used to run the youth group,* now works for a school across town.

In the first example, the adjective clause is essential because it identifies the subject. Without this information the reader would wonder who the person was. In the second example, the subject is identified by name. The adjective clause provides nonessential information about Mr. Greco.

Exercise 6.3

Put parentheses around each adjective clause. In the space provided write *E* if the clause is essential, or *NE* if it is nonessential. If the clause is nonessential, insert commas to separate it from the main clause. An example is done for you.

Example: __NE__ The recreation center, (which was redecorated by the youth group), is open six days a week.

_____ 1. Father Joseph who is the new youth director will help the group produce a play.

_____ 2. The play that was chosen requires both male and female actors who can sing.

_____ 3. Nick is working on **stagecraft** which includes lighting and set design.

_____ 4. The girl whom Nick has been dating will play a leading role.

_____ 5. The boy who was Nick's best friend will be the leading man.

Check your answers on page 100.

When to Use "Who," "Whom," "That" and "Which"

Use *who* or *whom* to stand for a person. *Who* can be used as the subject of a clause. *Whom* is only used as an object.

One way to decide between *who* and *whom* is to substitute the pronoun *he* or *him* (or *she* or *her*). *Who* is a subject (nominative) pronoun like *he* or *she*. *Whom* is an object pronoun like *him* or *her*.

Nick's father, (who had done some acting in high school), offered to help put on a **drama**, or play.

Who refers to *father* and serves as the subject of the clause. We could say "*he* had done some acting," so we use the subject pronoun, *who*.

Nick's father, (whom we all admired), had an easy sense of humor.

Whom also refers to *father*, but here it serves as the "object" that *we all admire*. We could have said "we all admired *him*," so we use the object pronoun, *whom*.

Use *that* or *which* to stand for an animal, thing, or idea. Generally, when the relative pronoun is used as a subject, *that* is used to introduce an essential clause, and *which* is used to introduce a nonessential clause.

Nick got into an argument (that involved stolen property).

The clause *that involved stolen property* is an essential part of this sentence. The subject of the clause is *that*.

The argument, (which involved stolen property), turned into a fistfight.

The argument (that involved stolen property) turned into a fistfight.

Here are two very similar sentences. In the first example, the adjective clause in nonessential. Its subject is *which*, and it is set off by commas. The focus of the sentence is on the argument becoming a fight. In the second example, the adjective clause is written as essential information; *that* is the subject, and no commas are used. This gives more weight to the cause of the argument.

Exercise 6.4

Fill in each blank with *who, whom, that,* or *which.* An example is done for you.

Example: The young man _who_ challenged Nick was not from the neighborhood.

1. Alonso claimed the stereo _____ the youth group used was stolen from him last month.

2. Actually, the stereo, _____ Father Joseph just bought at Green Electronics, did not even match Alonso's description.

3. Alonso gave Nick a shove _____ was returned with equal force.

4. Sophia called a police officer _____ she trusted.

5. The officer _____ responded was a stranger, though.

Check your answers on page 100.

Writing Assignments

Building Your Word Power

In your word notebook include the Key Terms and Life Skill Words from this chapter. Break each word into syllables or into word parts (prefixes, suffixes, and roots). Write an original sentence for at least five of the words.

Reading to Write

Think of a story, play, movie, or television drama you enjoyed. Explain how it made you think about something in your life or in the life of someone you know. First give the title and describe part of the story. Then explain how it reminded you of something from real life. Be sure to save your work in your portfolio.

Building Your Editing Checklist

Add the following items to the editing checklist that you began in Chapter 2:

- Use an adjective clause to express an idea that describes a noun in a main clause.
- Use commas to separate a nonessential adjective clause from a main clause.
- Do not separate an essential adjective clause from a main clause.
- Use *who* or *whom* to stand for people.
- Use *who* as a subject. Use *whom* as an object.
- Use *that* or *which* to stand for animals, things, or ideas.

Chapter 7

Complex Sentences with Adverbial Clauses

"This is the best one yet. Listen to this **restaurant review**," Eva said to her father, Julian Colon. "It's for a place on Fourth Street.

> For **elegant** dining on a budget we recommend *Costa Del Sol*. Owners Esther and Juan Santiago have created the atmosphere of a fine Spanish family restaurant without trendy frills or fancy prices. Serving Spanish, Portuguese, and Latin American specialties, the Santiagos offer **gourmet cuisine** that ordinary people can afford. While the **à la carte** menu boasts many tempting **entrées** and **appetizers, fixed price** dinners begin under $10 on week nights. A **gratuity** of 15% is added to your bill, but the service is so friendly that you may want to tip more. A dance band plays on weekends. **Reservations** are recommended for Friday or Saturday night.

"Do you think Amadeo would like it?"

"I wish you were planning to take me, instead of your husband!" Julian joked.

"It isn't *your* birthday," Eva said, smiling. "I wonder what they serve for $10," she thought out loud.

"Why not stop by and look at a menu? They sound friendly enough," Julian suggested.

Key Terms

- adverbial clause

Life Skill Words

- à la carte
- appetizer
- cuisine
- elegant
- entrée
- fixed price
- gourmet
- gratuity
- restaurant review
- reservation

The Job of an Adverbial Clause

In Chapter 6 you learned that an adjective clause is used to describe a noun. An **adverbial** (ad-VER-bee-uhl) **clause** is a dependent clause that describes a verb or adjective. An adverbial clause can tell about an action in terms of time, place, manner, condition, or reason.

In the examples that follow the adverbial clauses are shown in parentheses. The word or phrase in italics introduces the clause and links it to a verb of the main clause.

> *Time:* The <u>waiter</u> <u><u>will place</u></u> your order (*as soon as* <u>he</u> <u><u>returns</u></u> to the kitchen).

The adverbial clause tells *when* the waiter will place the order.

> *Place:* <u>We</u> <u><u>wanted to sit</u></u> (*where* <u>we</u> <u><u>could talk</u></u> privately).

The adverbial clause tells *where* we wanted to sit.

> *Manner:* The <u>busboy</u> <u><u>smiled</u></u> (*as if* his <u>job</u> <u><u>depended</u></u> on it).

The adverbial clause tells *how* (or *in what way*) the busboy smiled.

> *Condition:* <u>Amadeo</u> <u><u>will call</u></u> the waiter (*if* <u>he</u> <u><u>needs</u></u> assistance ordering).

The adverbial clause tells *why* (or *under what condition*) Amadeo will call the waiter.

> *Reason:* <u>We</u> <u><u>cannot offer</u></u> you the special fish (*because* <u>we</u> <u><u>have</u></u> no more).

The adverbial clause tells *why* (or *for what reason*) we cannot offer the fish.

An adverbial clause can answer the questions *how, when, where,* or *why.*

Exercise 7.1

In each clause underline the subject once and the verb twice. Put the adverbial clause in parentheses. Then draw an arrow from the introductory word or phrase to the verb it describes. An example is done for you.

Example: <u>We</u> <u><u>were seated</u></u> (*where* <u>we</u> <u><u>could see</u></u> the dance floor).

1. She spoke as if we had just met.

2. We will dance as soon as the band returns from its break.

3. We moved to the center of the empty dance floor, where everyone could see us.

4. She will let me lead if I insist.

5. We returned to our table because we wanted to order.

Check your answers on page 100.

Telling How

An adverbial clause can answer the question *how* about a verb or an adjective. The following words are commonly used to introduce such clauses: *as, as . . . as,* and *as if* or *as though.*

 Like other dependent clauses, an adverbial clause introduces ideas that depend on part of a main clause. The dependent clause may contain essential or nonessential information. A nonessential clause is set off from the main clause by a comma.

Main Idea:	The service was slow.
Dependent Idea:	You predicted it would be.
New Sentence:	The service was slow, (*as* you predicted).

The new sentence combines the two ideas. The adverbial clause tells *how* the service was. This nonessential information is set off by a comma since we already stated that the service was *slow.*

Alternate Sentence:	The service was *as* slow (*as* you predicted).

In this sentence the adverbial clause describes the adjective *slow,* telling *how slow* the service was. The *as . . . as* construction always surrounds an adjective—in this case, *slow*). The information in the clause is always essential, so no comma is used.

As if and *as though* have the same meaning. Both introduce a comparison that describes a verb. This information can be essential or nonessential.

Main Idea:	Eva danced wildly.
Dependent Idea:	She looked like a teenager.

New Sentence: Eva danced wildly, (*as if* [or *as though*] she were a teenager).

In this sentence *wildly* describes how Eva *danced*. The dependent clause also describes how she danced, but it is nonessential. A comma separates the clauses.

Alternate Sentence: Eva danced (*as if* [or *as though*] she were a wild teenager).

In this sentence the dependent clause alone describes *how* Eva *danced*. This essential information is not separated from the main clause.

Exercise 7.2

In each sentence put the adverbial clause in parentheses. Then draw an arrow from the introductory word or phrase to the verb it describes. Separate the dependent clause from the main clause with a comma if it provides nonessential information. An example is done for you.

Example: The food is excellent, (as the reviewer promised).

1. The fish was as tender as my grandmother made it.

2. The salad was crisp as the menu described.

3. The waiter carrying fresh rolls walked proudly as if he had baked them himself.

4. The chocolate cake was topped with ice cream as if calories meant nothing.

5. I felt as if I had died and gone to heaven.

Check your answers on page 101.

Lesson 3

Telling Why

An adverbial clause can describe the reasons or conditions for an action. In these cases it tells *why* about a verb. Words that commonly introduce reasons include *because, since,* and *so that.* A conditional clause begins with *if* or *unless.*

Main Idea:	Eva was willing to pay for this fancy dinner.
Reasons:	She loves Amadeo.
	Amadeo's birthday comes only once a year.
	She could show off for her friends.
New sentences:	Eva was willing to pay for this fancy dinner *because* she loves Amadeo.
	Eva was willing to pay for this fancy dinner *since* Amadeo's birthday comes only once a year.
	Eva was willing to pay for this fancy dinner *so that* she could show off for her friends.

As the first two new sentences show, *because* and *since* can be used interchangeably to introduce a reason. *So that* introduces a reason that may occur in the future.

Conditional clauses are introduced by *if* or *unless*.

Main Idea:	They may come back to this place.
Condition:	They have a good time.
New Sentence:	They may come back to this place *if* they have a good time.

If is used to introduce a positive condition. The main action will happen *if* the dependent condition is fulfilled.

Main Idea:	They will come back.
Condition:	The restaurant becomes too expensive.
New Sentence:	They will come back *unless* the restaurant becomes too expensive.

Unless is used to introduce a negative condition. The main action will happen *unless* the dependent condition is *not* fulfilled.

Exercise 7.3a

Each main idea is followed by a reason or condition. In the space provided combine the two clauses using the word or phrase shown. An example is done for you.

Example:	Main Idea:	They each ordered a glass of wine.
	Reason:	This was a special occasion.
	(because)	They each ordered a glass of wine because this was a special occasion.

1.	Main Idea:	Amadeo had to toast Eva loudly.
	Reason:	They were seated near the band.

(since) _____

_____

2. *Main Idea:*   He leaned over and spoke in her ear.
   Reason: She could hear him.
   (so that) _____

_____

3. *Main Idea:*   The band might play Eva's favorite song.
   Condition: Amadeo had the courage to ask.
   (if) _____

_____

4. *Main Idea:*   They lingered over coffee.
   Reason: They didn't want the night to end.
   (because) _____

_____

5. *Main Idea:*   They will stay until dawn.
   Condition: The restaurant closes.
   (unless) _____

_____

Check your answers on page 101.

Exercise 7.3b

For each main idea write a simple sentence that gives a reason or condition. Then use *because, since, so that, if,* or *unless* to combine the two clauses. An example is done for you.

Example: *Main Idea:*   The had to walk home.
            Reason: <u>The buses stopped running at 2 A.M.</u>
            <u>They had to walk home since the buses stopped running at 2 A.M.</u>

1. *Main Idea:*   They felt very close to each other.
   Reason: _____

_____

_____

2. *Main Idea:*   Amadeo would plan a surprise for Eva.

Condition: _____

_____

_____

3. *Main Idea:*   They would sleep late this morning.

Reason: _____

_____

_____

4. *Main Idea:*   Eva was glad for her father's advice.

Reason: _____

_____

_____

5. *Main Idea:*   Amadeo would recommend the restaurant to his friends.

Condition: _____

_____

_____

Telling When and Where

The following words introduce clauses that answer the question *when: after, as soon as, before, since, until, when, whenever,* and *while.*

Eva and Amadeo did not argue for a week (*after* [or *since*] they went out to dinner).

The dependent clause tells *when* they *did not argue.* Notice that *since* could be used in this sentence to mean *after.*

Words that tell *when* link two clauses in time. Of course, the time relationship depends on the choice of words.

Main Idea:	They felt very close to each other.
Time-related Idea:	They spent extra time together.

New Sentence: They felt very close *when* they spent extra time together.

New Sentence: They felt very close *after* they spent extra time together.

In the new sentences the words *when* and *after* link the two clauses. *When* generally means that the actions happen at the same time or on a continuing basis. *After* or *before* clearly places one event before another. You can express different meanings by choosing different linking words.

New Sentence: They felt very close *until* they spent extra time together.

In this example the relationship between the two ideas changes entirely.

Clauses can also be related in space. Use *where* to introduce a clause that locates an action in the main clause.

I will go (*where* I am welcome).

Exercise 7.4

Write a simple sentence that describes an event related to the main idea in time. Then use the word shown to combine the two clauses. An example is done for you.

Example: *Main Idea:* They had to walk home.

Time-related Idea: The buses stopped running.

(when) They had to walk home when the buses stopped running.

1. *Main Idea:* Amadeo helped Eva with the dishes.

   Time-related Idea: _____

   (after) _____

   _____

2. *Main Idea:* Amadeo would plan a surprise for Eva.

   Time-related Idea: _____

   (as soon as) _____

   _____

3. *Main Idea:* They would sleep late this morning.

   Time-related Idea: _____

   (after) _____

   _____

4. *Main Idea:* Eva was glad for her father's advice.

   Time-related Idea: _____

   (until) _____

   _____

5. *Main Idea:* Amadeo would recommend the restaurant to his friends.

   Time-related Idea: _____

   (whenever) _____

   _____

Using Commas with Dependent Clauses

Use a comma to separate the dependent clause from the main clause
- when the dependent clause comes first, or
- when it contains nonessential information.

Dependent clause first:	When the buses stopped running, Amadeo had to walk home.
Main clause first:	Amadeo had to walk home when the buses stopped running.

When the dependent clause comes first, it ends in a comma.

Essential:	I will walk down the street where I used to live.
Nonessential:	I will walk down Tremont Avenue, where I used to live.

When a dependent clause introduces extra information, separate it from the main clause with a comma.

Words That Introduce Adverbial Clauses

Question	Introductory Words
How?	as, as...as, as if, as though
Why?	
Reason	because, since, so that
Condition	if, unless
When?	after, as soon as, before, since, until, when, whenever, while
Where?	where

Exercise 7.5

In each clause, underline the subject once and the verb twice. Put the adverbial clause in parentheses. Then, draw an arrow from the introductory word or phrase to the verb that it describes. If necessary, separate clauses with a comma. An example is done for you.

Example: We were seated at our favorite table, (*where* we could see the dance floor).

1. As soon as the band returned our salads arrived.

2. The waiter placed the oil and vinegar tray where we could reach it easily.

3. We left our table for the dance floor where we could see the lively musicians.

4. Our meals will get cold unless we sit down to them now.

5. If I finish all this I won't be able to stand or dance again.

Check your answers on page 101.

Writing Assignments

Building Your Word Power

In your word notebook include the Key Terms and Life Skill Words from this chapter. Break each word into syllables or into word parts (prefixes, suffixes, and roots). Write an original sentence for at least five of the words.

Reading to Write

Clip or photocopy a review or advertisement of a restaurant. Write a complex sentence answering each of these questions:

- Where is it located?
- When might you go there?
- Why might you like it?
- Why might you dislike it?

Be sure to save your work in your portfolio.

Building Your Editing Checklist

Add the following items to the editing checklist that you began in Chapter 2:

- Use an adverbial clause to relate the action of a main clause to another idea that tells how, why, when, or where.
- When a dependent clause begins a sentence, end the clause with a comma.
- When a dependent clause gives extra, nonessential information, separate it from the main clause with a comma.

Chapter 8

Prepositional Phrases

Mustafah Berol surprised himself. He liked playing "nursemaid" to his cousins Aziza and Abdulla. Since his Aunt Samira worked nights on the **housekeeping** staff of the nursing home, it was up to Mustafah to get the kids off to school in the morning.

"Get dressed, you two!" he shouted from the kitchen to the giggling children in the back room. "Now what to make them for lunch . . . ," he wondered aloud.

Mustafah agreed to always pack a **balanced diet** for lunch. "They get enough junk as it is," Aunt Samira had sighed. Peanut butter sandwiches, carrot sticks, and graham crackers would be the menu for the day. With the milk served at school, that would cover all **four food groups**.

Aziza ran after Abdulla into the kitchen squealing, "Give me my shoes!"

"No, give *me* the shoes," said Mustafah sternly. "And what are you two wearing? We put those dirty things in the laundry last night!"

He heard himself sounding angry and quickly changed his tone.

"How will you ever develop a positive **self-image**, if you neglect your **wardrobe** and **hygiene**?" he said, imitating a fussy mother they had seen on TV. "Now eat your breakfast, and I'll choose something presentable," he continued, in a high-pitched voice.

Key Terms

- object of the preposition
- phrase
- preposition
- prepositional phrase

Life Skill Words

- balanced diet
- etiquette
- four food groups
- housekeeping
- hygiene
- manners
- self-image
- wardrobe

Lesson 1

Identifying Prepositions and Prepositional Phrases

A **preposition** (prehp-uh-ZIHSH-uhn) is a word that shows the relationship between a noun (or pronoun) and another noun, pronoun, or verb. A list of some common prepositions follows.

Some Common Prepositions

about	before	in	over
above	beside	into	through
across	between	of	to
after	by	on	under
among	during	opposite	with
around	for	out	within
at	from	outside	without

When these words act as prepositions, they often relate two nouns or pronouns in a sentence. Some of these words can be used in other ways, too.

Preposition: The cups hung *over* the plates.

Adverb: Breakfast was *over.*

In the first example, *over* relates *cups* and *plates.* We know the cups are over the plates. The plates are under the cups.

In the second example, *over* tells when *breakfast was.*

Preposition: He sat *opposite* her.

Noun: Whatever I say, he says the *opposite.*

In the first example, *opposite* relates *he* and *her.* The two people are facing each other.

In the second example, *opposite* means the thing (noun) that *he says.*

The word *to* is a common preposition. It is also used to introduce the most general form of a verb, called the *infinitive.*

Preposition: The sweater belonged *to* her.

Infinitive: I want *to go* home.

In the first example, *to* relates *her* and *sweater.* She owns the sweater.

In the second example, *to go* is the infinitive verb.

PREPOSITIONAL PHRASES

A **phrase** is a group of words without a subject and verb. A **prepositional** (prehp-uh-ZIHSH-shuhn-uhl) **phrase** begins with a preposition and ends with the noun or pronoun it addresses. That noun or pronoun is called the **object of the preposition**. Prepositional phrases are commonly used to add information to sentences.

In the following examples the prepositional phrase is in parentheses. The preposition is underlined once and the object of the preposition is underlined twice.

Aziza blew bubbles (<u>in</u> her <u><u>milk</u></u>).

In her milk tells where she blew the bubbles.

Abdulla made mountains (<u>of</u> <u><u>oatmeal</u></u>) (<u>in</u> his <u><u>bowl</u></u>).

Of oatmeal describes the mountains; *in his bowl* tells where those mountains were made.

Mustafah would give them a lesson (<u>in</u> table **<u><u>manners</u></u>**) (<u>at</u> snack <u><u>time</u></u>) (<u>after</u> <u><u>school</u></u>).

In table manners tells what kind of lesson; *at snack time* and *after school* tell when the lesson would be given.

Exercise 8.1a

The numbered sentences below contain eight (8) prepositional phrases. Put each prepositional phrase in parentheses. Underline the preposition once and the object of the preposition twice. An example is done for you.

Example: Mustafah smiled when his cousins walked (<u>in</u> the <u><u>door</u></u>).

1. He was dressed in his waiter's uniform.
2. "Walk right this way. Your table is waiting for you."
3. "On today's snack menu, we have ice cream, ice cream, and ice cream."
4. Abdulla and Aziza smiled at each other and ran to the table.
5. "And this snack comes with a free lesson in **etiquette** (EHT-ih-kuht)."
6. "Today, we will practice the rules of good table manners."

Check your answers on page 102.

USING PRONOUNS AS OBJECTS OF PREPOSITIONS

The noun that a preposition addresses is its object. You should only use object pronouns to replace a noun acting as an object of the preposition.

Pronouns to Use as Objects of Prepositions

Object Pronouns	Not Subject Pronouns
me	*not* I
him	*not* he
her	*not* she
us	*not* we
them	*not* they

You and *it* can be used as either subjects or objects.

Incorrect: Mustafah is doing his best for Abdulla and I.

Correct: Mustafah is doing his best (for Abdulla and *me*).

Abdulla and *me* are objects of the preposition *for.* You say *for me,* not *for I.*

Exercise 8.1b

Rewrite the following sentences replacing each underlined noun with the correct pronoun. Use subject pronouns for subjects and object pronouns for objects of the preposition. Underline the pronouns you choose. An example is done for you.

Example: "First," said Mustafah, "<u>Mustafah</u> will explain what good manners mean to <u>Mustafah</u>."

"First," said Mustafah, "<u>I</u> will explain what good manners mean to <u>me</u>."

1. "<u>Abdulla and I</u>," said Aziza, "don't want you to give a lecture to <u>Abdulla and Aziza</u>."

   _____

2. <u>Aziza and Abdulla</u> will have to watch Mustafah eat the ice cream without <u>Aziza and Abdulla</u>.

   _____

3. "<u>Abdulla</u> will listen to <u>Mustafah</u> without <u>Aziza</u>," protested Abdulla.

   _____

4. "<u>Abdulla</u> cannot listen without <u>Aziza</u>," said Aziza to her brother. "<u>Aziza</u> will listen to <u>Mustafah</u>, too."

   _____

5. "Please, Mustafah," smiled Aziza, "demonstrate for Abdulla and <u>Aziza</u> the proper way to eat ice cream."

_____

6. "Then you can get bowls for <u>Aziza</u> and for <u>Abdulla</u>," said Abdulla, "and <u>Aziza and Abdulla</u> will practice."

_____

Check your answers on page 102.

Prepositional Phrases as Adjectives

When prepositional phrases act as adjectives, they usually answer the questions _What kind of?_ or _Which one?_

adj.

Many families (with small children) ignore table manners.

With small children tells what kind of families.

adj.

The bowl (on the counter) is for you.

On the counter tells which bowl is for you.

Exercise 8.2

The five sentences below contain eight prepositional phrases. Put each prepositional phrase in parentheses. Then draw an arrow to the noun it modifies. Write _adj._ above the arrow to show it is used as an adjective. An example is done for you.

adj.

Example: This book (by Rachel Smith) says good manners show that you consider other people's feelings.

1. You may discuss the ingredients of the homemade soup.

2. Be sure that your ideas about the flavor of the gravy do not upset the cook.

3. Even if you are a guest of a friend, remember to praise the ordinary things about his home.

4. You might say, "I really like the cheery pattern of this tablecloth."

5. The person opposite you doesn't want to see the chewed food in your mouth while you talk.

Check your answers on page 102.

Prepositional Phrases as Adverbs

Although a preposition generally relates two nouns, that relationship often involves an action. When a prepositional *phrase* answers the question *Where? How?* or *When?* it acts as an adverb.

adv.
I passed the peas (to Samira).

The phrase *to Samira* tells *where* I passed the peas. The phrase tells about the action.

adv.
He spoke (in a gentle tone).

The phrase *in a gentle tone* tells *how* he spoke.

adv.
We listened politely (for several minutes).

The phrase *for several minutes* tells *when* we listened.

Exercise 8.3

Put each prepositional phrase in parentheses. Then draw an arrow to the verb it modifies. Write *adv.* above the arrow to show it is used as an adverb. An example is done for you.

adv.
Example: Mustafah planned the surprise dinner (for Saturday).

1. The table was set with matching dishes.

2. Flowers were arranged beside the mirror.

3. Fresh bread cooled on the window sill.

4. Samira sat in her favorite chair.

5. The children placed their napkins on their laps.

6. Aziza dropped her spoon under the table.

7. She requested another with a polite question.

8. Mustafah tossed the salad with two large forks.

9. Abdulla said a prayer before they ate.

10. Both children helped clear the table after dinner.

Check your answers on page 103.

Misplaced Modifiers

Generally your readers will expect modifiers (adjectives and adverbs) to tell about a word nearby. A misplaced prepositional phrase can cause confusion.

> *Confusing:*   Samira opened the door for the woman and children with a bundle of laundry.

In the example we are not sure what is happening. Were the children carrying the bundle together? Did Samira open the door with a bundle of laundry?

> *Clearer:*   Samira opened the door for the children and the woman with a bundle of laundry.

Here we know that the woman had the bundle of laundry. Samira opened the door for the children and her.

Always try to put an adjective or adverb close to the word it describes. You may need to rewrite a sentence entirely.

> *Confusing:*   I think someone accidentally dropped the fish I cooked in the garbage.

Here it seems the fish was cooked in the garbage!

Clearer: The fish is missing. I think someone accidentally dropped it in the garbage.

Here the prepositional phrase *in the garbage* clearly refers to *it*, meaning *the fish*.

Exercise 8.4

In the space provided, rewrite each sentence so that it clearly expresses the meaning shown. An example is done for you.

Example: The girl opened the bag of cookies with a toothy smile.
(*Meaning:* The girl had the smile.)
Clearer: The girl with a toothy smile opened the bag of cookies.

1. Here are some suggestions for avoiding junk food from our dentist.
(*Meaning:* The suggestions came from the dentist.)

   _____

   _____

2. One of Aziza's friends was referred to the guidance counselor with a bad attitude.
(*Meaning:* The friend had the bad attitude.)

   _____

   _____

3. Aziza ran to her mother with torn pants in tears.
(*Meaning:* Aziza's pants were torn, and she was crying.)

   _____

   _____

4. Abdulla asked for a book from the teacher with a big smile.
(*Meaning:* Abdulla was smiling.)

   _____

   _____

5. Aziza rode her bicycle while I was sleeping on the street without permission.
(*Meaning:* Aziza rode in the street.)

   _____

   _____

Check your answers on page 103.

Building Your Word Power

In your word notebook include the Key Terms and Life Skill Words from this chapter. Break each word into syllables or into word parts (prefixes, suffixes, and roots). Write an original sentence for at least five of the words.

Reading to Write

Clip or photocopy an article about caring for children. Consider such topics as manners, discipline, healthy food, and care of clothing.

1. Mark the prepositional phrases in the article, and draw arrows to the words they modify.
2. Explain three ideas from the article in three separate sentences.

Be sure to save your work in your portfolio.

Building Your Editing Checklist

Add the following items to the editing checklist that you began in Chapter 2:

- Use prepositional phrases to add information to sentences.
- Place prepositional phrases near the words they modify.

Chapter 9

Punctuation of Phrases, Clauses, and Quotations

Andrea Monroe knocked on the door across the hall, and her neighbor, Samira Berol, answered.

"Do you have a minute?" Andrea asked. "I need to start Maya in school, so I hoped you could tell me what you did when Aziza started."

"Oh, there's nothing to it," Samira smiled. "Come in and we'll have some coffee."

As she got the cups, Samira explained that you **register** your child at the local elementary school. The secretary in the main office had the forms and would help Andrea fill them out.

"The school wants to know your address and telephone number and the name of anyone who is **authorized** to pick up Maya after school," Samira remembered. "You would be giving the school **permission** to let Maya go with that person."

"Oh, and you can use me as your **emergency** contact," Samira continued. "If you're stuck at work, Mustafah or I can pick her up. Aziza likes to play with Maya."

"And *you* can use *me*," Andrea offered.

"Great!" said Samira. "One more thing, though. Before she starts, you have to get Maya **vaccinated**—you know, **immunized** against childhood diseases."

"Uh, oh. Maya isn't going to like getting another shot," Andrea laughed. "I've been using the clinic in the hospital. I hope these vaccinations are the last ones she'll need for a while."

Key Terms

- appositive
- direct quotation
- indirect quotation
- noun phrase
- quotation mark
- subject phrase

Life Skill Words

- authorize
- curriculum
- emergency
- immunize
- permission
- register
- vaccinate

Subject Phrases and Appositives

As you learned in chapters 6 and 7, commas are used to separate nonessential clauses in a sentence. Essential information is *not* set off by commas. This is true for phrases too.

A group of words that acts as a subject is called a **subject phrase.** Since a subject is essential to a sentence, a subject phrase is *not* set off by commas.

> *Her longtime neighbor* asked Samira's advice.
>
> *One of her concerns* was registering her daughter for school.

The subject phrases *her longtime neighbor* and *one of her concerns* are *not* separated from their verbs with commas.

A **noun phrase** is a group of words including a noun and its modifiers. (A subject phrase is a type of noun phrase.) Sometimes a noun or a noun phrase is used to identify the noun or pronoun that comes right before it. Such an identifier, which is called an **appositive,** is nonessential to the meaning of a sentence. Appositives are set off by commas.

> Andrea, *her longtime neighbor,* asked Samira's advice.
>
> Mustafah, *Samira's nephew,* was not home.

The phrases *her longtime neighbor* and *Samira's nephew* are appositives. Each one identifies the noun that comes right before it (*Andrea* and *Mustafah*). These appositives are not essential to the meaning of either sentence, so they are separated by commas.

An appositive can identify a subject or an object.

> Smith Elementary School, *the oldest school in the district,* was around the corner from Andrea's home, *Langston Apartments.*

The subject, *Smith Elementary School,* is identified by the appositive *the oldest school in the district.* The object of the preposition, *home,* is identified by the appositive *Langston Apartments.*

An appositive may be a proper name or a descriptive phrase.

> The school's secretary, *Ms. Winterbottom,* explained the forms.
>
> Mrs. Levine, *the principal of the school,* introduced herself to Maya.

A comma, of course, represents a pause. When an appositive forms a single unit with the noun it identifies, it is *not* set off by commas. There would be no pause when you read the following sentence aloud.

Her *daughter Maya* would be five years old this summer.

The phrase *daughter Maya* acts as a single unit of thought. The words are not separated by commas, and they are read without pause.

Her daughter, *Maya,* would be five years old this summer.

My friend, *Joe,* helped me fill out the forms.

Her husband, *John,* walked their daughter to school.

Strictly speaking, *Maya, Joe,* and *John* are appositives. Commas are used to separate them from the words that they identify. Your reader will pause at each comma. Perhaps you want your reader to think of *Maya* and not another daughter. Perhaps you want to put special emphasis on *Joe* or *John.*

Exercise 9.1

In the following sentences cross out misplaced commas. Add needed commas. Underline appositives. An example is done for you.

Example: Mustafah's friend, <u>Bill</u>, <u>an aide at Smith School</u>, showed Andrea and Maya the kindergarten classrooms.

1. The classroom with the best view of the courtyard, was used by Ms. Hickey an experienced teacher.
2. The newest teacher Mr. Guido had not yet decorated his classroom the one nearest the main office.
3. One of Maya's favorite activities, singing was a big part of the **curriculum** the skills taught at that school.
4. Teachers used oak tag a stiff paper to make badges for each child to color.
5. Maya told her cousin, Daryl, all about her school tour and about her newest friend Bill.

Check your answers on page 103.

Commas in Compound Sentences

You learned in Chapter 3 that a compound sentence is made of two or more independent clauses joined by a conjunction (*and, but,* or *or*). Each *independent clause* includes a subject and verb and expresses a complete thought. The clauses in a compound sentence must be logically related, of course. You use a comma before the conjunction when you join independent clauses.

Independent clause + *Comma* + *Conjunction* + Independent clause

Samira has two children,	*but*	Andrea has just one.
The teacher loves children,	*and*	they love her.
You should register early,	*or*	you may get caught in the fall rush.

In each example, notice that the two independent clauses express related ideas. A conjunction joins these two complete thoughts. A comma ends the first clause. When you read these sentences aloud, you will notice a natural pause at that point.

The conjunctions *and, but,* or *or* may be used to join two verbs of a single subject. In that case, do *not* use a comma before the conjunction. The words that follow do not express a complete thought.

Mustafah walks his cousins to school *and* continues on to work.

In this simple sentence, a single subject, *Mustafah,* performs two actions, *walks* and *continues.* No comma is used, since *continues on to work* is not a complete thought.

Exercise 9.2

Match the beginnings and endings of the sentences below so that they make sense. Rewrite these sentences in the spaces provided. Be sure to use commas to separate complete thoughts. An example is done for you.

Beginnings

Example: Andrea took her daughter to the store

1. Maya wanted the one with cartoon characters
2. Maya looked at new shoes
3. The school serves breakfast and lunch
4. Maya and Aziza play school
5. Maya may nap in the afternoon
6. Andrea is gaining a schoolgirl

Endings

or she may play quietly on her bed.

but Andrea won't buy them until winter.

and Andrea bought it for her.

or go to the park on Saturdays.

and Maya can get these meals for free.

and Maya picked out a new notebook.

but losing her baby.

Example: <u>Andrea took her daughter to the store, and Maya picked out</u>
<u>a new notebook.</u>

1._____

_____

2._____

_____

3._____

_____

4._____

_____

5._____

_____

6._____

_____

Check your answers on page 103.

Commas in Complex Sentences

As you learned in Chapter 2, a *complex sentence* contains both a dependent and independent (or main) clause. The dependent clause does not express a complete thought by itself. Dependent clauses can act as adjectives (Chapter 6) or as adverbs (Chapter 7).

Use these three rules to punctuate complex sentences correctly:

- Generally, do *not* use a comma to separate a main clause from a dependent clause.

- When a dependent clause begins a sentence, however, end the clause with a comma.

- When a dependent clause gives extra, nonessential information, separate it from the main clause with a comma.

Maya was ready *when the school year began.*

The dependent clause follows the main clause, so no comma is needed.

When the school year began, Maya was ready.

Since the dependent clause begins the sentence, it ends in a comma.

Maya, *who prepared all summer,* was ready for school.

The dependent clause, which interrupts the subject and verb of the main clause, provides nonessential information and is set off by commas.

Maya was ready for school *because she prepared all summer.*

The clauses are not separated by commas since the dependent clause provides information essential to the meaning of the sentence.

Exercise 9.3

Combine each beginning clause with another clause below so that they make sense as sentences. Rewrite these sentences in the spaces provided. Use commas to separate clauses only when necessary. An example is done for you.

Beginning Clauses

Example: When Maya got her immunization shot

1. The shot was given at a free clinic
2. The school required proof of vaccination
3. If children are not vaccinate
4. Polio killed and crippled millions of young adults.
5. Vanessa refused to have her baby vaccinated
6. She may have a problem with the authorities

Other Clauses

they may get sick and spread sickness to others

which prevented several diseases

before the vaccine was available

before a child enrolled

she bit her lip but did not cry

who believed in only natural medicines

when the child reaches school age

Example: <u>When Maya got her immunization shot, she bit her lip but did not cry.</u>

1. _____

_____

2. _____

_____

3. _____

_____

4. _____

_____

5. _____

_____

6. _____

Check your answers on page 103.

Quotations within a Sentence

You may use a person's words within a sentence directly or indirectly.

DIRECT QUOTATIONS

Quotation marks (" ") can be used to set off someone's exact words. A **direct quotation** can come from a written source or from speech. The introductions to the chapters of this book contain many examples of quotations of dialogue between people.

"Do you have a minute?" Andrea asked.

Do you have a minute? are Andrea's exact words, so they are enclosed in quotation marks.

You can use a phrase like *Andrea asked* or *he said* to identify the speaker. When the quotation begins a sentence, place a comma or other punctuation within the quotation marks before the identifying phrase.

"Oh, there's nothing to it," Samira smiled.

A comma separates the quotation from the identifying phrase. The comma comes before the closing quotation mark.

The identifying phrase can interrupt the quotation. In that case, separate the interrupting phrase with commas. Again, punctuation at the end of a quotation is placed before the closing mark.

"Come in," Samira said, "and we will have some coffee."

The first part of the quotation ends in a comma, and so does the identifying phrase.

When the interrupted quotation is a single sentence, begin its second part with a lowercase letter. In the example above *and* is not capitalized.

When you use an identifying phrase to interrupt a quotation, place it between two main parts of the quotation. You may place it after the subject phrase, after the first clause, or after the first sentence. The quotation in the example above is a compound sentence.

"(Come in)," Samira said, "and (we will have some coffee)."

The interrupting phrase is placed between the clauses, shown here in parentheses.

When a quotation ends a sentence, the final punctuation is placed within the closing quotation mark.

Samira continued, "You can use me as your emergency contact."
Samira shouted, "You can use me as your emergency contact!"
Samira asked, "Can you use me as your emergency contact?"

A period, exclamation point, or question mark can end both the quotation and the sentence.

INDIRECT QUOTATIONS

When you want to rearrange or restate a person's exact words, use an **indirect quotation.** An indirect quotation tends to emphasize the content of the message instead of the speaker.

Indirect quotations are usually introduced with the words if, whether, or that.

Original:	Andrea asked Samira, "Could I use you as an emergency contact?"
Restatement:	Andrea asked *if* [or *whether*] she could use Samira as an emergency contact.

Here, the original question is rewritten as a statement without quotation marks. Notice that no question mark is used when if or whether introduces the restatement.

Original:	Andrea asked Samira, "Could I use you as an emergency contact?"
	"Sure, go right ahead," Samira said.
Rearrangement:	Samira said *that* Andrea could use her as an emergency contact.

Here, the exact words are rearranged. Again, no quotation marks are used.

Exercise 9.4

Rewrite each quotation three different ways: (a) with an identifying phrase at the beginning of the sentence, (b) with an identifying phrase that interrupts the quotation, and (c) as an indirect quotation. An example is done for you.

Example: Andrea to Maya: You will like kindergarten.

Identifier, quotation: <u>Andrea said to Maya, "You will like kindergarten."</u>

Identifier interrupting quotation: <u>"You," Andrea said to Maya, "will like kindergarten."</u>

Indirect quotation: <u>Andrea told Maya that she would like kindergarten.</u>

1. Aziza to Maya: School is fun because we sing songs.

   Identifier, quotation: _____

   _____

   Identifier interrupting quotation: _____

   _____

   Indirect quotation: _____

   _____

2. Maya to Aziza: Do you play with blocks?

   Identifier, quotation: _____

   _____

   Identifier interrupting quotation: _____

   _____

   Indirect quotation: _____

   _____

3. Samira to Andrea: The girls play together like sisters.

Identifier, quotation: _____

_____

Identifier interrupting quotation: _____

_____

Indirect quotation: _____

_____

4. Andrea to Samira: They are better than sisters. Sisters would fight!

Identifier, quotation: _____

_____

Identifier interrupting quotation: _____

_____

Indirect quotation: _____

_____

Check your answers on page 104.

Writing Assignments

Building Your Word Power

In your word notebook include the Key Terms and Life Skill Words from this chapter. Break each word into syllables or into word parts (prefixes, suffixes, and roots). Write an original sentence for at least five of the words.

Building Your Writing Power

Choose one of the following topics or one of your own. Research the topic by interviewing friends or experts, or by gathering written material about it. Then write at least five sentences about what you learn. Try to include appositives and quotations. Check your use of commas.

Be sure to save your work in your portfolio.

- Requirements for registering students in public school.
- Volunteering to help in the classroom.
- Making a special request of a school on behalf of a child.
- Working with a school to deal with a child's behavior problem.

Building Your Editing Checklist

Add the following items to the editing checklist that you began in Chapter 2:

- Do *not* separate a subject phrase from its verb with a comma.
- Use commas to separate appositives from the nouns or noun phrases they identify.
- Use a comma before the conjunction to separate independent clauses.
- Use a comma at the end of a dependent clause that begins a sentence.
- Use commas to separate a nonessential clause from the rest of a sentence.
- Use commas to separate identifying phrases from direct quotations.
- Place punctuation within quotation marks.

Chapter 10

Parallel Structure

"Andrea, this is like a gift from heaven," said Julian Alvarez. "All summer you've wanted to get out of the city. Now my cousin needs someone to share a cabin on a lake, and you 'don't know?'"

"Look, I've never been camping, and I don't know your cousin. Besides, how am I going to afford it?" Andrea Monroe worried aloud.

"First of all, it's not exactly camping. It's a **bungalow.** You know, like a little house. And it's really cheap. It's in a **state park,** so they use some tax money to keep the price down. My cousin Pedro said you and Maya could have a bedroom for the week for $100."

"Well, what about food? We can't afford to eat out all week," Andrea said, hoping to be convinced.

"Pedro's old station wagon will get us to town for groceries. There's a kitchen in the cabin—*and* a bathroom, too!"

"Well, there had better be a bathroom!" Andrea said, grinning.

"Pedro said he was thinking about **booking** a **tent platform** instead of a cabin, but his girlfriend Bonita wanted indoor plumbing, too," Julian said, laughing.

"Has he been there before, or is he just trusting some **brochure**?" Andrea asked suspiciously.

"Why don't you come over for dinner tomorrow. Pedro and Bonita will be there. We can talk it over then," Julian suggested. It was best to give Andrea a little time to think it over.

Key Terms

- bulleted list
- correlative conjunction
- numbered list
- parallel structure
- stem
- sublists

Life Skill Words

- booking
- brochure
- bungalow
- state park
- tent platform

Lists within Sentences

To make your writing clear, express similar ideas using the same format. This is called **parallel structure.**

Wrong: Julian is *handsome* and a *talented painter,* too.

This sentence tells two things about Julian. He is *handsome* and he is a *talented painter. Handsome* is an adjective, but *talented painter* is a noun phrase. These two items should be parallel, since they appear in the same sentence and are connected to the same subject by the same verb.

Right: Julian is *a handsome man* and a *talented painter,* too.

Here, two noun phrases are used to describe Julian. Notice that these phrases have the same structure and serve the same purpose in the sentence.

Wrong: Julian likes *fishing, to laugh,* and *root beer.*

This sentence presents a list of things that Julian likes. The three items in the list should be parallel.

Right: Julian likes *fishing, laughing,* and *drinking root beer.*

Here the items are all expressed as actions ending in *-ing.*

Right: Julian likes to *fish, laugh,* and *drink root beer.*

Here the items are all expressed as actions in the infinitive form *(to fish, to laugh, to drink).* Notice that the word *to* can be used once to introduce all three of the verbs in the list.

Right: Julian likes *fishing, laughter,* and *root beer.*

Here the items are all expressed as things—nouns. Notice that some *-ing* words like *fishing* can be used as actions (verbs) or activities (nouns).

Rewrite each sentence making the items in italics parallel. Underline the parallel items in your new sentence. An example is done for you.

Example: Andrea wants to escape *the heat* and *smelling the garbage*.
Andrea wants to escape <u>the heat</u> and the <u>smelly garbage</u>.

1. Maya has never been *fishing* or *to row* before.

   _____

2. Andrea wondered about *what to pack, insect spray,* and *to drive at night.*

   _____

3. Andrea asked Bonita about *sharing a kitchen* and *split the food expenses.*

   _____

4. Pedro was *relaxed* and a *good friend.*

   _____

5. Maya asked about *bears, seeing ghosts,* and *campfires.*

   _____

6. Andrea was *a fun-loving person* but *nervous.*

   _____

Check your answers on page 104.

Numbered and Bulleted Lists

Items in a list of instructions, questions, or ideas may be quite long. To make these ideas clear to the reader, you may write them on separate lines. Items in a **numbered list** begin with a number. Items in a **bulleted list** begin with a dark circle, or other symbol, called a *bullet.*

A list often begins with part of a sentence called a **stem.** A stem usually ends with a colon (:). The items in the list should have the same structure, and they should logically connect to the stem.

Weak:	You should take a vacation:

1. because you deserve one,
2. It's cheap.
3. Maya needs to see something green for a change.

Better:	You should take a vacation because:

1. You deserve one.
2. It's cheap.
3. Maya needs to see something green for a change.

The stem in the better list includes the word *because*, since each item connects to that word. Notice that each item completes the stem. Items are capitalized and punctuated consistently, too.

Generally use a numbered list when the order of items is important, or when you want to refer to the items by number. Use a bulleted list when order and reference don't matter. The list above could be bulleted instead of numbered.

Or:	Some reasons you should take this vacation are:

- You deserve it.
- You can afford it.
- Your daughter needs a change of scene.

Notice that each item is a reason. Each reason is expressed as a sentence. Items can be single words, phrases, clauses, or sentences, but they should all have the *same* structure.

A list can outline a great deal of information and serve as an introduction or a summary for a longer piece of writing. List items can contain **sublists,** or lists of their own. The following examples show two ways of creating sublists. As always, you should use the same format for each list item.

Run-in Sublist

Vacation activities:
- On the waterfront: fishing, boating, swimming.
- In the country: hiking, picnicking, climbing.
- Around the cabin: reading, playing cards, loafing.

Notice that each list item begins with a prepositional phrase (*on the waterfront, in the country, around the cabin*). The sublist items follow a colon. They are all -*ing* words, and they are separated by commas. Each item ends in a period.

Freestanding Sublist

Vacation activities:
1. On the waterfront
   - fishing
   - boating
   - swimming

2. In the country
   - hiking
   - picnicking
   - climbing
3. Around the cabin
   - reading
   - playing cards
   - loafing

A freestanding sublist gives you more room to add information if you are planning a longer piece of writing.

Exercise 10.2

Rewrite each paragraph as a stem and list. Make sure the items flow from the stem and that all items have the same structure. Capitalize and punctate consistently. Number items when order or importance matter. Bullet items when order does not matter. You can leave out some details, but include all major items. An example is done for you.

Example: (Andrea writes:) I have some reasons for skipping this vacation, too. First, I've never been away with Julian. Second, I hardly know Pedro, and I just met Bonita. Third, there would be no little kids for Maya to play with.

Reasons to skip this vacation:

1. I've never been away with Julian.
2. I don't know Pedro or Bonita well.
3. Maya would have no playmates.

1. (Julian writes:) This is my plan for convincing Andrea to go on vacation. First, I'll get Pedro to invite Samira and her kids to rent the fourth bedroom. Then, I'll offer to pay for Samira's and Andrea's groceries. Finally, I'll ask Samira to talk Andrea into coming.

   _____

   _____

   _____

   _____

2. (From the State Park Department's brochure:) To get from New City to Dutch Elm Park, take Spruce Highway east to Exit 5, Route 512, North. Follow signs to Elmont and turn left at the light in the center of town onto Green Avenue. Continue 4.5 miles to the park entrance on the right.

_____

_____

_____

_____

3. (Andrea wrote:) I'll need to take lots of stuff for the kitchen on this vacation. We'll need a large frying pan, a sauce pan, and a kettle. We'll also need cooking utensils like a spatula, ladle, long-handled spoon, and a colander to drain spaghetti. We'll need a cutting board and knives. And we'll need eight plates, bowls, cups, forks, spoons, and knives. (Hint: Use sublists.)

_____

_____

_____

_____

4. (Julian wrote:) I'll have to remember to do a few things before we go away. The rent is due. I have to stop the mail so it doesn't pile up. I have to clean the refrigerator and put out the garbage, so the place doesn't stink when I get back. And I have to find someone to take care of my cat. (Hint: Leave out some details.)

_____

_____

_____

_____

Check your answers on page 104.

Parallel Form with Correlative Conjunctions

As you know, *conjunctions* join words, phrases, and clauses. **Correlative conjunctions** are paired conjunctions like *both . . . and, either . . . or, neither . . . nor, not only . . . but also,* and *whether . . . or.* The items they join should be in parallel form.

Wrong:	Julian not only <u>enjoys fishing</u> but also <u>swimming</u>.
Right:	Julian enjoys not only <u>fishing</u> but also <u>swimming</u>.

You can think of this sentence as a very short list. The stem, *Julian enjoys*, applies to both list items, *fishing* and *swimming*. The correlative conjunctions join items in the same form.

Wrong:	Today we are going both <u>to the lake</u> and <u>town</u>.
Right:	Today we are going to both <u>the lake</u> and <u>the town</u>.

Wrong:	I'll be happy whether <u>we go rowing</u> or <u>just sit around</u>.
Right:	I'll be happy whether <u>we go rowing</u> or <u>we just sit around</u>.

Exercise 10.3

Rewrite the following sentences so the elements joined by correlative conjunctions have parallel form. An example is done for you.

Example: During the car trip, Maya would neither <u>take a nap</u> nor would she <u>sit quietly</u>.

During the car trip, Maya would neither take a nap nor sit quietly.

1. Samira is not only <u>grateful as a friend</u> but also <u>as a mother</u>.

_____

_____

2. Before the trip Pedro collected rent both <u>from Julian</u> and <u>Samira</u>.

_____

_____

3. For dinner Andrea would either <u>cook fresh fish</u> or <u>she would prepare a big salad</u>.

_____

_____

4. Julian wondered whether <u>they would arrive by lunchtime</u> or much <u>later</u>.

_____

_____

5. Andrea not only <u>cooked dinner</u> but <u>she cleaned up afterward</u>.

_____

_____

Check your answers on page 104.

Writing Assignments _____

Reading to Write

Gather information about using public resources like state parks, recreation areas, and historical sites. Brochures may be available in your library or from your state government. (Check the blue pages of your telephone book for state departments under headings like *Recreation, Parks,* or *Environmental Protection.*)

Assignment: After reading the information you gathered do the following:

- Make a list of locations and activities that interest you.
- Write a few sentences describing one public recreation resource.
- Rewrite directions to one location in list form.

Check your work for parallel structure. Be sure to save your work in your portfolio.

Building Your Editing Checklist

Add the following items to the editing checklist that you began in Chapter 2:

- Express similar ideas using parallel structure.
- Write a stem for a list that can introduce every item.
- Be sure each list item has the same form.
- Use parallel form for words or phrases joined by correlative conjunctions.

Answer Key

Chapter 1

Exercise 1.1

1. F
2. S
3. S
4. F
5. F
6. S
7. S
8. F
9. S
10. F

Exercise 1.2a

1. Safety
2. chart
3. Alaska
4. lifeguards
5. Happiness
6. information
7. painters
8. City Hall
9. kindness
10. concert

Exercise 1.2b

1. The library <u>installed</u> new shelves.
2. Tony <u>registered</u> to vote today.
3. Boston <u>is</u> a famous American city.
4. Her thoughtfulness <u>made</u> that manager popular.
5. Cindy <u>checked</u> the phone book first.
6. The employees <u>agreed</u> to leave on time.
7. Our neighbors <u>traveled</u> 800 miles by bus.
8. The newcomers <u>hated</u> the cold weather.
9. Savona <u>applied</u> for a job.
10. Impatience when standing in a long line <u>is</u> understandable.

Exercise 1.3

1. TC
2. OK
3. OK
4. OK
5. TC
6. TC
7. TC
8. OK
9. TC
10. OK

Exercise 1.4a

1. Applying
2. OK
3. OK
4. OK
5. All
6. But
7. Do
8. Show
9. Anna
10. OK

Exercise 1.4b

1. EXC
2. DEC
3. INT
4. DEC
5. DEC
6. EXC
7. INT
8. IMP
9. DEC
10. EXC

Exercise 1.4c

1. period
2. period - Give
3. question mark
4. period
5. exclamation point
6. question mark - How
7. period
8. period - Most
9. exclamation point
10. question mark

Chapter 2

Exercise 2.1

Answers may vary. Sample answers:
1. fragment - Verb is missing. - What did they do?
2. fragment - Subject is missing. - Who spoke?
3. sentence
4. fragment - Verb (and probably a thought completer) is missing. - What about the bulletin board?
5. fragment - Subject is missing. - What seemed half empty?
6. sentence
7. fragment - Thought completer is missing. - How did the notice look?
8. fragment - Subject is missing. - Who discussed the phone system?
9. sentence
10. fragment - Thought completer is missing. - What about the "star key"?

Exercise 2.2 a

Answers will vary. Sample answers:
1. The instructions were long.
2. Jaime felt the brass doorknob.
3. Sentence
4. His voice sounded hoarse.
5. The library director saw her reflection in the window.

Exercise 2.2 b

Answers will vary. Sample answers:
1. The library's reference desk shone.
   The library's reference desk was crowded.
2. The huge dictionary on the wooden stand tilted.
   The huge dictionary on the wooden stand cost $150.
3. The newspaper reporter observed.
   The newspaper reporter asked tough questions.
4. The children playing basketball scattered.
   The children playing basketball looked tired.
5. Jaime's dog, Ralph, barked.
   Jaime's dog, Ralph, was a beagle.

Exercise 2.3

Answers will vary. Sample answers:
1. Charlie had heard the carnival parade around the corner.
2. The musicians were carrying banners and flags.
3. We set up the food booths.
4. The band played music in the street until dark.
5. I have eaten more than I should have.

Exercise 2.4

Answers will vary. Sample answers:
1. Because the voice mail system offered a long list of options, Jaime got confused.
2. Since Jaime got confused, he hung up.
3. Although Jaime was patient, he was annoyed about the wasted phone call.
4. If Jaime called back, he would be charged for another call.
5. He got a paper and pencil before he called back.
6. Since he pressed the "2" key, he reached the department that he needed.
7. When Jaime finally spoke to a live person, he felt happier.
8. After Jaime hung up, he thought about his first experience with voice mail.
9. "I would have walked to the library if I had known all this would happen," he thought.
10. I'd rather talk to a live person—although, when I wrote down the options, I could get voice mail to work.

Chapter 3

Exercise 3.1

1. <u>Either Vivian or Shyrone</u> <u>will carry</u> the packages home.
2. <u>Emery and Shyrone</u> <u>live</u> near the bus stop.
3. <u>Both Emery and Shyrone</u> <u>like</u> listening to live music.
4. <u>Emery or Shyrone</u> <u>was starting</u> to speak.
5. <u>Emery and I</u> <u>were grinning.</u>

Exercise 3.2

Answers will vary. Sample answers:

1. The <u>brakes</u> of the truck behind them <u>squealed</u> but <u>failed.</u>
2. The <u>passengers</u> all <u>looked</u> back and <u>screamed.</u>
3. The <u>truck</u> <u>might stop</u> in time or <u>crash</u> into the bus.
4. <u>Emery</u> <u>bumped</u> into the elderly woman and <u>hit</u> his head on the luggage rack.
5. The elderly <u>woman</u> <u>groaned</u> or <u>mumbled</u> something.

Exercise 3.3

1. sped, failed to signal, and ran
2. chased and pulled (no comma)
3. shouted, cursed, and left
4. Neither Ned nor Rick
5. Reporters, pedestrians, and police officers

Exercise 3.4

Answers may vary. Sample answers:

1. The ten-trip fare card cost $22.50, and Shyrone bought one.
2. To get to work she took the N2 bus, and then she transferred to the AA bus.
3. The whole trip took 45 minutes, but the time passed quickly.
4. She could keep taking the bus to work, or she could start taking the train.
5. The train was faster, but it was more expensive.

Exercise 3.5

Answers may vary. Sample answers (correction strategy):

1. The city transportation department has a telephone line to help people. Using a complex system of buses and trains can be confusing. (a: Form separate sentences.)
2. Vivian took the bus, but she preferred the train. (c: Create a compound sentence.)
3. The man didn't buy a ticket. He jumped over the entrance barrier and boarded the train. (a & b: Rewrite as two sentences.)
4. She didn't get off at the library; she went all the way to Elmer Avenue. (d: Use a semi-colon.)
5. The driver looked at the rear axle, and a mechanic examined the engine. (c: Create a compound sentence.)

Chapter 4

Exercise 4.1a

1. The <u>Derbys</u> <u>get</u>
2. <u>Sally</u> <u>shops</u>
3. <u>They</u> <u>smell</u>
4. <u>Michael</u> <u>misses</u>
5. The easy <u>chair</u> <u>reminds</u>
6. Now <u>you</u> <u>cook</u>
7. <u>Michael and his father</u> <u>eat</u>
8. <u>I</u> <u>write</u>
9. The <u>package</u> <u>arrives</u>.
10. <u>It</u> <u>touches</u>

Exercise 4.1b

1. <u>They</u> <u>get</u> a few sympathy cards each day.
2. <u>She</u> <u>shops</u> for flowers.
4. <u>He</u> <u>misses</u> his aunt.
5. <u>It</u> <u>reminds</u> him of her.
7. <u>They</u> <u>eat</u> together most evenings.
9. <u>It</u> <u>arrives</u> early in the day.

Exercise 4.2

Subjects and verbs are correct as shown. Answers will vary. Sample answers:

1. <u>You</u> <u>had</u> your chance.
2. <u>Robert</u> <u>has</u> a cold.
3. <u>They</u> <u>are waiting</u> for their friends.
4. <u>We</u> <u>have sold</u> the old rug.
5. <u>I</u> <u>am</u> afraid to go out alone.
6. <u>You</u> <u>were</u> my friend.
7. <u>Susan</u> <u>has</u> a bicycle.
8. <u>It</u> <u>is standing</u> on the front steps.
9. <u>She</u> <u>has left</u> the lights on.
10. <u>I</u> <u>have</u> a red raincoat.

Exercise 4.3

1. <u>Neither he nor his father</u> <u>needs</u> the exercise.
2. <u>Either the package or the letters</u> <u>are</u> waiting for them.
3. <u>Neither the letter carrier nor her note</u> <u>has</u> said for sure.
4. <u>Not only the men but also the girls</u> <u>were</u> anxious for the delivery.
5. <u>Mary and Jill</u> <u>wait</u> impatiently at home.

Exercise 4.4

1. This <u>sheet</u> ~~of stamps~~ <u>contains</u> five sets of four wildflowers.
2. The <u>publication</u> ~~of a new stamp design~~ <u>is</u> called an issue.
3. The <u>subjects</u> ~~of a commemorative issue~~ <u>are</u> being honored.
4. <u>Heroes</u> ~~of the Civil War~~ <u>were</u> honored by a recent commemorative issue.
5. Several <u>inventors</u>, ~~as well as one scientist,~~ <u>were</u> featured on a series of stamps.

Exercise 4.5

Rewrites will vary. Suggested answers:
1. There <u>is</u> only one <u>clerk</u> behind the counter.
   Rewrite: One clerk is working behind the counter.
2. There <u>is</u> a <u>woman</u> tapping her foot impatiently.
   Rewrite: A woman is tapping her foot impatiently.
3. There <u>are</u> two little <u>boys</u> leaning on the display case.
   Rewrite: Two little boys are leaning on the display case.
4. There <u>is</u> a friendly <u>customer</u> chatting with the clerk.
   Rewrite: A friendly customer is chatting with the clerk.
5. There <u>are</u> several <u>people</u> fidgeting and mumbling in line.
   Rewrite: Several people are fidgeting and mumbling in line.

Chapter 5

Exercise 5.1

1. <u>Each</u> <u>was</u> reviewed by a newspaper.
2. <u>Neither</u> <u>has</u> started on time.
3. <u>Much</u> <u>was</u> said about this film.
4. <u>One</u> <u>plays</u> all day and night.
5. <u>Another</u> <u>sounds</u> good to me.

Exercise 5.2

1. <u>Another</u> of those scenes <u>has</u> me on the edge of my seat.
2. Every <u>one</u> of the actors <u>is</u> so handsome.
3. <u>Much</u> of these movies <u>was</u> devoted to car chases.
4. <u>Neither</u> of those people <u>is</u> keeping quiet.
5. <u>Each</u> of those G-rated cartoons <u>pleases</u> children.

Exercise 5.3a

1. <u>More</u> than one customer <u>has</u> walked out.

2. <u>Most</u> of the popcorn <u>is</u> buttered.

3. <u>Most</u> of the posters <u>are</u> above eye level.

4. <u>None</u> of the theater <u>is</u> quiet.

5. <u>None</u> of the actors <u>are</u> talented.

6. <u>More</u> of the scenes <u>have</u> "adult situations."

7. <u>Some</u> of the coming attractions <u>look</u> interesting.

8. <u>All</u> of the soda <u>is</u> gone.

9. <u>Some</u> of the people <u>have</u> fallen asleep.

10. <u>Any</u> of the ushers <u>look</u> bored.

Exercise 5.3b

1. <u>Few</u> <u>hold</u> my attention like that one.
2. <u>None</u> of those films <u>are</u> worth seeing.
3. <u>Each</u> of the movies <u>was</u> a hit.
4. <u>More</u> of the box offices <u>sell</u> reserved seats now.
5. <u>Any</u> of those nude scenes <u>make</u> the film R-rated.
6. <u>Some</u> of that strong language <u>bothers</u> me.
7. <u>One</u> of my favorite stars <u>has</u> retired in poor health.
8. <u>Several</u> in this film <u>have</u> been seen on TV.
9. <u>Either</u> of those seats <u>is</u> good enough.
10. <u>Most</u> of my friends <u>talk</u> about movies.

Exercise 5.4

Rewrites will vary. Suggested answers:
1. The movie <u>club</u> <u>meets</u> once a month.
2. The <u>choir</u> <u>are</u> fighting over solo selections.
   Rewrite: <u>Members</u> of the choir <u>are</u> fighting over solo selections.
3. The cub scout <u>den</u> <u>have</u> worked hard for their merit badges.
   Rewrite: The cub <u>scouts</u> in this den <u>have</u> worked hard for their merit badges.
4. The <u>government</u> <u>is</u> cutting taxes and services.
5. The <u>jury</u> <u>have</u> argued over the evidence for two days.
   Rewrite: The <u>jurors</u> <u>have</u> argued over the evidence for two days.
6. An <u>army</u> <u>moves</u> on its stomach.
7. The <u>committee</u> <u>were</u> debating the plan.
   Rewrite: The <u>members</u> of the committee <u>were</u> debating the plan.
8. The <u>flock</u> <u>lands</u> on the lake like a single bird.
9. The football <u>team</u> <u>were</u> struggling with their homework.
   Rewrite: Our football <u>players</u> <u>were</u> struggling with their homework.
10. The <u>company</u> <u>is</u> going to open another store.

Chapter 6

Exercise 6.1

1. The <u>tapes</u> (<u>that</u> <u>were borrowed</u>) <u>sounded</u> modern.

2. <u>Gina</u>, (<u>who</u> <u>was</u> Nick's mother), <u>looked</u> into the recreation hall.

3. The <u>hall</u>, (<u>which</u> <u>was converted</u> from an old hardware store), <u>belonged</u> to the church.

4. <u>Sal</u> <u>watched</u> the video (<u>that</u> <u>coached</u> youth center volunteers).

5. The <u>video</u> <u>focused</u> on the theme of respect, (<u>which</u> <u>is</u> the key to a successful social organization).

Exercise 6.2

1. <u>He</u> <u>checked</u> with teachers at the school (that <u>most</u> of the kids <u>attended</u>).

2. At the library, <u>Sal</u> <u>searched</u> for materials in the card catalog, (which <u>Mr. Jefferson</u> <u>explained</u> to him).

3. <u>Mr. Jefferson</u>, (whom <u>Sal</u> <u>respected</u>), <u>recommended</u> several high-interest books of fiction for the youth group's library.

4. <u>Sal</u> <u>convinced</u> Nick to organize the group's science fiction comic books, (which many <u>members</u> <u>had read</u> and <u>scattered</u>).

5. <u>Sal</u> <u>worked</u> with Father Joseph, (whom <u>he</u> <u>trusted</u>).

Exercise 6.3

NE	1.	Father Joseph, (who is the new youth director), will help the group produce a play.
E, E	2.	The play (that was chosen) requires both male and female actors (who can sing).
NE	3.	Nick is working on stagecraft, (which includes lighting and set design).
E	4.	The girl (whom Nick has been dating) will play a leading role.
E	5.	The boy (who was Nick's best friend) will be the leading man.

Exercise 6.4

1. that   2. which   3. that   4. whom   5. who

Chapter 7

Exercise 7.1

1. <u>She</u> <u>spoke</u> (as if <u>we</u> <u>had</u> just <u>met</u>).

2. <u>We</u> <u>will dance</u> (as soon as the <u>band</u> <u>returns</u> from its break).

3. We moved to the center of the empty dance floor, (where everyone could see us).

4. She will let me lead (if I insist).

5. We returned to our table (because we wanted to order).

Exercise 7.2

1. The fish was as tender (as my grandmother made it).

2. The salad was crisp, (as the menu described).

3. The waiter carrying fresh rolls walked proudly, (as if he had baked them himself).

4. The chocolate cake was topped with ice cream, (as if calories meant nothing).

5. I felt (as if I had died and gone to heaven).

Exercise 7.3a

1. Amadeo had to toast Eva loudly since they were seated near the band.
2. He leaned over and spoke in her ear so that she could hear him.
3. The band might play Eva's favorite song if Amadeo had the courage to ask.
4. They lingered over coffee because they didn't want the night to end.
5. They will stay until dawn unless the restaurant closes.

Exercise 7.5

1. (As soon as the band returned), our salads arrived.

2. The waiter placed the oil and vinegar tray (where we could reach it easily).

3. We left our table for the dance floor, (where we could see the lively musicians).

4. Our <u>meals</u> <u>will get</u> cold (unless <u>we</u> <u>sit</u> down to them now).

5. If <u>I</u> <u>finish</u> all this, (<u>I</u> <u>won't be able</u> to stand or dance again).

Chapter 8

Exercise 8.1a

1. He was dressed (<u>in</u> his waiter's <u>uniform</u>).
2. "Walk right this way. Your table is waiting (<u>for</u> <u>you</u>)."
3. "(<u>On</u> today's snack <u>menu</u>), we have ice cream, ice cream, and ice cream."
4. Abdullah and Aziza smiled (<u>at</u> each <u>other</u>) and ran (<u>to</u> the <u>table</u>).
5. "And this snack comes (<u>with</u> a free <u>lesson</u>) (<u>in</u> <u>etiquette</u>)."
6. "Today, we will practice the rules (<u>of</u> good table <u>manners</u>).

Exercise 8.1b

1. "<u>We</u>," said Aziza, "don't want you to give a lecture to <u>us</u>.
2. <u>They</u> will have to watch Mustafah eat the ice cream without <u>them.</u>
3. "<u>I</u> will listen to <u>you</u> without <u>her</u>," protested Abdulla.
4. "<u>You</u> cannot listen without <u>me</u>," said Aziza to her brother. <u>I</u> will listen to <u>him</u>, too.
5. "Please, Mustafah," smiled Aziza, "demonstrate for Abdulla and <u>me</u> the proper way to eat ice cream."
6. "Then you can get bowls for <u>her</u> and for <u>me</u>," said Abdulla, "and <u>we</u> will practice."

Exercise 8.2

1. You may discuss the ingredients (of the homemade soup).

2. Be sure you ideas (about the flavor) (of the gravy) do not upset the cook.

3. Even if you are a guest (of a friend), remember to praise the ordinary things (about his home).

4. You might say, "I really like the cheery pattern (of this tablecloth)."

5. The person (opposite you) doesn't want to see the chewed food (in your mouth) while you talk.

Exercise 8.3

1. The table was set (with matching dishes). *adv.*

2. Flowers were arranged (beside the mirror). *adv.*

3. Fresh bread cooled (on the window sill). *adv.*

4. Samira sat (in her favorite chair). *adv.*

5. The children placed their napkins (on their laps). *adv.*

6. Aziza dropped her spoon (under the table). *adv.*

7. She requested another (with a polite question). *adv.*

8. Mustafah tossed the salad (with two large forks). *adv.*

9. Abdulla said a prayer (before they ate). *adv.*

10. Both children helped clear the table (after dinner). *adv.*

Exercise 8.4

Answers will very. Suggested answers:
1. Here are some suggestions from our dentist for avoiding junk food.
2. One of Aziza's friends with a bad attitude was referred to the guidance counselor.
3. With her pants torn, Aziza ran in tears to her mother.
4. With a big smile, Abdulla asked for a book from the teacher.
5. While I was sleeping, Aziza rode her bicycle on the street without permission.

Chapter 9

Exercise 9.1

1. The classroom with the best view of the courtyard, was used by <u>Ms. Hickey</u>, <u>an experienced teacher</u>.
2. The newest teacher, <u>Mr. Guido</u>, had not yet decorated his classroom, <u>the one nearest the main office</u>.
3. One of Maya's favorite activities, <u>singing</u>, was a big part of the curriculum, <u>the skills taught at that school</u>.
4. Teachers used oak tag, <u>a stiff paper</u>, to make badges for each child to color.
5. Maya told her cousin, <u>Daryl</u>, all about her tour and about her newest friend, <u>Bill</u>.

Exercise 9.2

Answers may vary. Suggested answers.
1. Maya wanted the one with cartoon characters, and Andrea bought it for her.
2. Maya looked at new shoes, but Andrea won't buy them until winter.
3. The school serves breakfast and lunch, and Maya can get these meals for free.
4. Maya and Aziza play school or go to the park on Saturdays.
5. Maya may nap in the afternoon, or she may play quietly on her bed.
6. Andrea is gaining a schoolgirl but losing her baby.

Exercise 9.3

Answers may vary. Suggested answers:
1. The shot, which prevented several diseases, was given at a free clinic.
2. The school required proof of vaccination before a child enrolled.
3. If children are not vaccinated, they may get sick and spread sickness to others.

4. Polio killed and crippled millions of young adults before the vaccine was available.
5. Vanessa, who believed in only natural medicines, refused to have her baby vaccinated.
6. She may have a problem with the authorities when the child reaches school age.

Exercise 9.4

Answers may vary. Suggested answers:

1. Identifier, quotation: Aziza said to Maya, "School is fun because we sing songs."
Identifier interrupting quotation: "School is fun," Aziza told Maya, "because we sing songs."
Indirect quotation: Aziza told Maya that school was fun because they sing songs.
2. Identifier, quotation: Maya asked Aziza, "Do you play with blocks?"
Identifier interrupting quotation: "Do you," Maya asked Aziza, "play with blocks?"
Indirect quotation: Maya asked Aziza if (or *whether*) she played with blocks.
3. Identifier, quotation: Samira said to Andrea, "The girls play together like sisters."
Identifier interrupting quotation: "The girls," Samira said to Andrea, "play together like sisters."
Indirect quotation: Samira told Andrea that the girls play together like sisters.
4. Identifier, quotation: Andrea told Samira, "They are better than sisters. Sisters would fight!"
Identifier interrupting quotation: "They are better than sisters," Andrea told Samira. "Sisters would fight!"
Indirect quotation: Andrea told Samira that the girls played together better than sisters because sisters would fight!

Chapter 10

Exercise 10.1

Answers will vary. Suggested answers:

1. Maya has never been <u>fishing</u> or <u>rowing</u> before.
2. Andrea wondered about <u>packing</u>, <u>getting insect spray</u>, and <u>driving at night</u>.

3. Andrea asked Bonita about <u>sharing a kitchen</u> and <u>splitting the food expenses</u>.
4. Pedro was a <u>relaxed person</u> and a <u>good friend</u>.
5. Maya asked about <u>bears</u>, <u>ghosts</u>, and <u>campfires</u>.
6. Andrea was <u>fun-loving</u> but <u>nervous</u>.

Exercise 10.2

Answers will vary. Suggested answers:

1. To convince Andrea to go on vacation:
    1. Get Pedro to invite Samira and her kids.
    2. Offer to pay for Samira's and Andrea's groceries.
    3. Ask Samira to convince Andrea.
2. Directions from New City to Dutch Elm Park:
    1. Take Spruce Highway east to Exit 5, Route 512, North.
    2. Follow signs to Elmont.
    3. Turn left at the light in the center of town onto Green Avenue.
    4. Continue 4.5 miles to the park entrance on the right.
3. Kitchen equipment for vacation:
    * Pots: frying pan, sauce pan, kettle
    * Cooking utensils: spatula, ladle, long-handled spoon, colander
    * Cutting equipment: cutting board, knives
    * Table settings for eight: plates, bowls, cups, forks, spoons, knives.
4. Things to do before vacation:
    * Pay rent.
    * Stop mail.
    * Clean refrigerator.
    * Put out garbage.
    * Arrange cat care.

Exercise 10.3

1. Samira is grateful not only <u>as a friend</u> but also <u>as a mother</u>.
2. Before the trip, Pedro collected rent from both <u>Julian</u> and <u>Samira</u>.
3. For dinner, Andrea would either <u>cook fresh fish</u> or <u>prepare a big salad</u>.
4. Julian wondered whether <u>they would arrive by lunchtime</u> or <u>they would arrive much later</u>.
5. Andrea not only <u>cooked dinner</u> but also <u>cleaned up afterwards</u>.

à la carte (ah-luh-kahrt) *adjective* According to a restaurant menu that prices items separately.

adjective clause (AJ-ihk-tihv klawz) *noun* A dependent clause that describes a noun or pronoun.

adverbial clause (ad-VER-bee-uhl klawz) *noun* A dependent clause that describes a verb or adjective.

alphabetical order (al-fuh-BEHT-uh-kuhl OHR-duhr) *noun* A system for arranging names, words, or things starting with the letter *a* and ending with the letter *z.*

analyzed (AH-nuh-leyezd) *verb* Thought over the choices available.

antecedent (an-tuh-SEED-uhnt) *noun* A noun that a pronoun replaces or refers to.

appetizer (AHP-puh-teye-zuhr) *noun* A food or drink served before a meal to stimulate the appetite.

appositive (uh-PAHZ-uh-tihv) *noun* A noun or a noun phrase that identifies the noun or pronoun right before it.

authorize (AW-thuh-reyez) *verb* To give power to. To give permission.

balanced diet (BAL-uhnst DEYE-uht) *noun* Food selected (usually from the *four food groups*) to give the right mix of things your body needs to grow and stay healthy.

blue pages (bloo PAY-jehz) *noun* Blue-colored pages positioned in the back of a telephone book that list in alphabetical order local, state, and federal government agencies or departments.

booking (BOOK-ihng) *verb* Reserving.

box office (bahks OHF-ihs) *noun* A small windowed section at the front of a theater to sell tickets.

brochure (broh-SHOOR) *noun* A small pamphlet or booklet.

bulleted list (BUHL-uh-tuhd lihst) *noun* A list whose items begin with a dark circle or other symbol called a *bullet.*

bungalow (BUN-guh-loh) *noun* A one-storied house with a low-pitched roof. A cabin.

capitalize (KAP-eh-tuhl-eyez) *verb* To write or print the first letter of a word in a capital letter.

card catalog (kahrd KAH-tuh-lawg) *noun* A reference tool consisting of an index card for each work in a library by title, subject, and author. The cards are stored alphabetically in drawers.

catalog (KAH-tuh-lawg) *noun* A list, index, or register.

certified mail (SUHR-tuh-feyed mayl) *noun* Regular mail that has been labeled with a recorded number that can be used to trace the item if it is lost.

collective noun (koh-LEHK-tihv nown) *noun* A word representing a group of people, animals, or things.

comma splice (KAWM-uh spleyes) *noun* The incorrect use of a comma to link independent clauses.

commemorative stamp (kuh-MEHM-ruh-tihv stamp) *noun* A postal stamp that honors the person or subject shown.

community bulletin board (kuh-MYOO-nuh-tee BUHL-uh-tuhn bawrd) *noun* A listing of activities and events in a community.

complex sentence (KUHM-plehks SEHN-tuhns) *noun* A group of words expressing a complete thought and containing both a dependent and independent clause.

compound sentence (KAHM-pownd SEHN-tuhns) *noun* A sentence made of two or more independent clauses joined by a conjunction (*and, but,* or *or*).

compound subject (KAHM-pownd SUB-jehkt) *noun* Two or more nouns or pronouns acting as the subject of a sentence.

compound verb (KAHM-pownd verb) *noun* Two or more verbs that apply to the same subject.

conjunction (kuhn-JUNK-shuhn) *noun* A word, like *and, but,* and *or,* used to join words and clauses.

conjunction pair (kuhn-JUNK-shuhn pair) *noun* A pair of words, like *both...and, either...or,* and *neither...nor,* used together to join words or clauses.

correlative conjunction (kuh-REH-lay-tihv kuhn-JUNK-shuhn) *noun* Word pairs, like *both...and, either...or, neither...nor, not only...but also,* and *whether...or,* used to join words, phrases, and clauses.

cuisine (kwih-ZEEN) *noun* A style of cooking.

curriculum (kuh-RIH-kyoo-luhm) *noun* The courses or skills taught by a school.

declarative sentence (duh-KLAIR-uh-tihv SEHN-tuhns) *noun* A sentence that states (or declares) a fact.

departments (deh-PAWRT-mehnts) *noun* Divisions of a government agency.

dependent clause (deh-PEHN-duhnt klawz) *noun* A group of words that contains a subject and a verb but does not express a complete thought.

direct object (duh-REHKT OHB-jehkt) *noun* A noun or pronoun that a subject acts upon.

direct quotation (duh-REHKT kwoh-TAY-shuhn) *noun* An exact reproduction of someone's words.

discount (DIHS-kownt) *noun* A reduced cost.

drama (DRAHM-uh) *noun* A play on stage, television, or film.

editing (EHD-uh-tihng) *verb* Improving something written.

editing checklist (EHD-uh-tihng CHEHK-lihst) *noun* A list of things to look for when rereading and improving something you wrote.

elegant (EHL-ih-guhnt) *adjective* Marked by tasteful richness and high quality.

emergency (ih-MER-jehn-see) *noun* An unforeseen situation that calls for immediate action.

entrée (AHN-tray) *noun* The main dish of a meal.

essential clause (ih-SEHN-shuhl klawz) *noun* A dependent clause that cannot be omitted without changing the meaning of the main clause.

etiquette (EHT-ih-kuht) *noun* Standards of behavior recognized as polite.

exclamatory sentence (ehks-KLAM-uh-taw-ree SEHN-tuhns) *noun* A sentence that expresses a strong emotion or surprise.

extension (ehks-STEHN-shuhn) *noun* An extra telephone connected to a main line.

fare card (fair kard) *noun* A card good for a number of trips or a certain amount of money in a public transportation system.

fiction (FIHK-shuhn) *noun* Something invented. A story.

fixed price (fihkst preyes) *noun* The price charged for a special set of complete meals in a restaurant.

four food groups (fawr food groops) *noun* Four categories of foods from which to choose a balanced diet: dairy products, meat and protein-rich products, fruits and vegetables, and grains and starches.

fragment (FRAHG-muhnt) *noun* A group of words that does not express a complete thought.

G rating (jee RAY-tihng) *noun* A movie rating that means the film is appropriate for all (or *General*) audiences.

gourmet (GOOR-may) *adjective* Appealing to people who appreciate fine food and drink.

government (GU-vuhrn-muhnt) *noun* The local, state, or state group or organization that has the authority (usually by being elected) to make and enforce laws.

government guide (GU-vuhrn-muhnt geyed) *noun* A publication on colored (usually blue) pages at the end of a telephone book that lists in alphabetical order local, state, and federal goverment agencies or departments.

gratuity (gruh-TOO-uh-tee) *noun* A tip. A small payment as thanks for good service.

helping verb (HEHL-pihng verb) *noun* A verb placed before the main verb that helps change the tense.

housekeeping (HOWSE-keep-pihng) *noun* The routine tasks done to keep a household or system working properly.

hygiene (HEYE-jeen) *noun* Conditions or practices that support good health.

immunize (IH-myoo-neyez) *verb* To protect from disease. To vaccinate.

imperative sentence (ihm-PEHR-uh-tihv SEHN-tuhns) *noun* A sentence that expresses a command or an order.

indefinite pronoun (ihn-DEHF-ih-niht PROH-nown) *noun* A word that stands for a noun, but does not identify its antecedent specifically. Indefinite pronouns include: *another, each, every, either, neither, much, one, both, few, many, several, all, any, more, most, none, some.*

independent clause (ihn-duh-PEHN-duhnt klawz) *noun* A group of words containing a subject and a verb that can stand alone as a sentence.

indirect quotation (ihn-duh-REHKT kwoh-TAY-shuhn) *noun* A restated or rearranged statement of someone's words.

information (ihn-fawr-MAY-shuhn) *noun* Knowledge from study or instruction.

insured mail (ihn-SHOORD mayl) *noun* Mail which, if lost, results in the postal service paying the owner its stated value. Higher value items cost more to insure.

interlibrary loan (ihn-tuhr-LEYE-brair-ee lohn) *noun* A loan of materials between libraries.

interrogative sentence (ihn-ter-RAHG-uh-tihv SEHN-tuhns) *noun* A sentence that expresses a question.

issue (IHSH-oo) *noun* The publication of a new stamp design.

library (LEYE-brair-ee) *noun* 1. A place where books, music, films, and reference materials are kept and often lent to the public. 2. A collection of publications on the same topic.

main clause (mayn klawz) *noun* An independent clause in a complex sentence.

manners (MAN-uhrz) *noun* Habits of behavior.

mileage charge (MEYE-lihj charj) *noun* A taxi cab's charge for every part of a mile traveled.

movie listing (MOO-vee LIHST-ihng) *noun* A written collection of movie theaters, the movies they are showing, and the times of each showing.

movie rating (MOO-vee RAY-tihng) *noun* An indication of the age of the appropriate audience for a movie. Movies that contain strong language, violence, or sexual scenes are rated for older audience.

movie review (MOO-vee rih-VYOO) *noun* A report about a movie that gives selected details to support the writer's opinion.

nonessential clause (NAHN-ih-sehn-shuhl klawz) *noun* A dependent clause that can be omitted without changing the meaning of the main clause.

noun phrase (nown frayz) *noun* A group of words including a noun and its modifiers.

numbered list (NUM-buhrd lihst) *noun* A list whose items begin with numbers.

object of the preposition (OHB-jehkt uv thuh preh-puh-ZIH-shuhn) *noun* The noun or pronoun addressed by a preposition.

option (OHP-shuhn) *noun* A choice, especially in a voice mail system, such as various departments within a particular agency or organization.

parallel structure (PAR-uh-lehl STRUK-chuhr) *noun* Matching written formats used to express similar ideas.

permission (puhr-MIH-shuhn) *noun* The act of allowing or authorizing.

PG rating (pee-gee RAY-tihng) *noun* A movie rating that means *Parental Guidance* is recommended for younger viewers who may find these films too intense.

PG-13 rating (pee-gee thuhr-TEEN RAY-tihng) *noun* A movie rating that means *Parental Guidance* is recommended for viewers between 13 and 17 who may find these films too intense. Children under 13 are not admitted without an adult.

phrase (frayz) *noun* A group of words without a subject and verb.

plan (plan) *noun* A project or a program.

plural (PLOOR-uhl) *adjective* Representing more than one item.

portfolio (pawrt-FOH-lee-oh) *noun* A collection of writing, notes, and information, often stored in a notebook or folder.

postal service (POHS-tuhl SUHR-vuhs) *noun* A self-supporting government agency that delivers letters and packages to all locations in the country. It also prints and sells stamps that can be used to pay the delivery fee.

pound key (pownd kee) *noun* A key on a telephone number pad for the symbol "#."

predicate (PREH-dih-kuht) *noun* A group of words in a clause that includes the verb and its thought completer.

predicate adjective (PREH-dih-kuht AJ-ihk-tihv) *noun* An adjective in the predicate that describes the subject.

predicate nominative (PREHD-ih-kuht NAHM-nuh-tihv) *noun* A noun or pronoun that names, identifies, or stand for the subject.

preposition (preh-puh-ZIH-shuhn) *noun* A word that shows the relationship between a noun (or pronoun) and another noun, pronoun, or verb.

prepositional phrase (prehp-uh-ZIHSH-uh-nuhl frayz) *noun* A group of words that begins with a preposition and ends with the noun or pronoun it addresses.

public transportation (PUH-blihk trans-pawr-TAY-shuhn) *noun* Transportation systems such as bus, train, taxi, and ferry systems that carry the public, usually for a fee.

publicity (puh-BLIH-suh-tee) *noun* Advertising. Public attention.

punctuation mark (puhnk-chuh-WAY-shuhn mahrk) *noun* Marks that break up written language, like the period (.), comma (,), exclamation point (!), and question mark (?).

quotation marks (kwoh-TAY-shuhn mahrks) *noun* Punctuation marks ("") that surround a direct quotation.

R rating (ar RAY-tihng) *noun* A movie rating that means the film is *R*estricted to adults and children accompanied by adults.

reference desk (REH-fuhr-ehns dehsk) *noun* A location in a library where a staff member helps people find information and materials.

register (REH-juh-stuhr) *verb* To enroll or sign up —as a voter or student.

registered mail (REH-uh-stuhrd mayl) *noun* Mail that is numbered for tracing, travels under lock and key, and is signed for each time it changes hands.

relative pronoun (REH-luh-tihv PROH-nown) *noun* A pronoun whose gender and number depend on its antecedent: *who, whose, whom, which, that*. Relative pronouns can be used to introduce dependent clauses.

reservation (reh-zuhr-VAY-shuhn) *noun* An arrang-ement to hold a seat at a restaurant or theater.

restaurant review (REHS-turh-rahnt rih-VYOO) *noun* A report about a restaurant that describes the food, prices, service, and atmosphere to support the writer's opinion.

return address (rih-TUHRN uh-DREHS) *noun* The address of the sender of a letter or package, used by the postal service to return the item if the adressee cannot be found.

return receipt (rih-TUHRN ruh-SEET) *noun* A receipt mailed back to the sender when a letter or package is signed for.

run-on sentence (RUN-ahn SEHN-tuhns) *noun* A group of words that contains two or more complete thoughts that are not clearly related, separated, or connected.

schedule (SKEH-dyool) *noun* A timetable. A list of events and times.

science fiction (SEYE-uhns FIHK-shuhn) *noun* A story that involves imagined inventions and tools.

self-image (sehlf-IH-mihj) *noun* A person's idea of himself or herself.

semicolon (SEH-mih-koh-luhn) *noun* A punctuation mark (;) used in place of a conjunction in a compound sentence.

sentence (SEHN-tuhns) *noun* A group of words that express a complete thought.

singular (SIHNG-yoo-luhr) *adjective* Representing one item.

stagecraft (STAYJ-kraft) *noun* The skillful use of the elements needed to put on a play, including lighting, scenery, direction, and so on.

star key (stahr kee) *noun* A key on a telephone number pad for the symbol "*."

state park (stayt pahrk) *noun* A park run by the state government.

stem (stehm) *noun* A clause or phrase that introduces a list.

subject (SUB-jehkt) *noun* The part of a sentence that names a person, a place, a thing, an idea, or a feeling.

subject phrase (SUB-jehkt frayz) *noun* A noun phrase acting as the subject of a clause.

subject-verb agreement (SUB-jehkt—verb uh-GREE-muhnt) *noun* The condition where the subject and verb of a sentence have the same "number." Singular subjects must match singular verbs. Plural subjects must match plural verbs.

sublists (SUHB-lihsts) *noun* Lists within lists.

taxi meter (TAK-see MEE-tuhr) *noun* A device that measures the time and distance charges for a taxi cab ride.

telephone book (TEH-luh-fohn book) *noun* A book that includes names, addresses, and telephone numbers of individuals and businesses.

tent platform (tehnt PLAHT-fawm) *noun* A wooden platform on which you pitch a tent.

thought completer (thawt kuhm-PLEET-uhr) *noun* A word or group of words that completes the meaning of a sentence.

timetable (TEYEM-tay-buhl) *noun* A schedule. A list of events and times.

trace (trays) *verb* To follow the path of someone or something (such as mailed package).

training video (TRAYN-ihng VIH-dee-oh) *noun* A videotaped recording of material designed to teach a specific skill.

transfer (TRANS-fuhr) *noun* A ticket that lets you continue your trip on another bus, train, etc, usually in the same direction and within the same zone.

vaccinate (VAHK-suh-nayt) *verb* To inject with a virus in order to make a person immune.

verb (verb) *noun* 1. The part of a sentence that tells you something about the subject. 2. The part of a sentence that expresses a physical action, a mental action, or a feeling. 3. The part of a sentence that makes a statement about the subject.

verb phrase (verb frayz) *noun* A group of words including a main verb and a helping verb.

voice mail (vois mayl) *noun* A message that you can record or hear by telephone.

wardrobe (WAWRD-rohb) *noun* 1. A collection of clothing. 2. A piece of furniture for storing clothing.

zone (zohn) *noun* An area within a public transportation system.